FAITH FUSION

Knowing, Loving, and Serving Christ in the Catholic Church

Gloria Shahin

with

David M. Dziena

Rev. George T.M. Hafemann

Includes Revised Order of Mass +

Foreword by

Rev. Alfred McBride, O.Praem.

The Subcommittee on the Catechism, United States Conference of Catholic Bishops, has found this catechetical text, © 2010, to be in conformity with the Catechism of the Catholic Church.

OurSundayVisitor

Our Sunday Visitor Publishing Division
Huntington, Indiana

Doctrinal Reviewer: Rev. Alfred McBride, O.Praem.
Reviewers/Consultants: Leisa Anslinger, Matthew Bunson, Heidi Busse, Marie Scanlon, Dorothy Vogt
Cover Design, Interior Design and Photo Research: Lindsey Riesen

Nihil Obstat
Rev. Michael Heintz, Ph.D.
Censor Librorum

Imprimatur
✠ John M. D'Arcy
Bishop of Fort Wayne-South Bend
November 4, 2009

The *Nihil Obstat* and *Imprimatur* are official declarations that a book or pamphlet is free of doctrinal and moral error. No implication is contained therein that those who have granted the *Nihil Obstat* and *Imprimatur* agree with the contents, opinions, or statements expressed.

Write:
Our Sunday Visitor Publishing Division
Our Sunday Visitor, Inc.
200 Noll Plaza
Huntington, Indiana 46750
1-800-348-2440
bookpermissions@osv.com

Acknowledgments
Scripture texts used in this work are taken from the *New American Bible*, copyright © 1991, 1986, and 1970 by the Confraternity of Christian Doctrine, Washington, DC 20017 and are used by permission of the copyright owner. All rights reserved.

Excerpts from the *Catechism of the Catholic Church*, second edition, copyright © 2000, Libreria Editrice Vaticana-United States Conference of Catholic Bishops, Washington, DC 20017. Used with permission. All rights reserved.

Excerpts from the English translation for *Lectionary for Mass* © 1969, 1981, 1997, International Committee on English in the Liturgy Corporation. (ICEL); excerpts from the English translation of *Rite of Baptism for Children* © 1969, ICEL; excerpts from the English translation of *Rite of Penance* © 1974, ICEL; excerpts from the English translation of *Rite of Marriage* © 1969, ICEL; excerpts from the English translation of *Rite of Confirmation (Second Edition)* © 1975, ICEL; excerpts from the English translation of *A Book of Prayers* © 1982, ICEL; excerpts from the English translation of *The Roman Missal* © 2010, ICEL. All rights reserved.

ISBN: 978-1-59276-593-5
Inventory No. X875

Cover Image: The Crosiers
Illustrations not listed are from Shutterstock
Catechism cover courtesy of USCCB.

IMAGE CREDITS
TABLE OF CONTENTS: Page 1: Shutterstock – top; **Shane Johnson Illustrations** – middle; **The Crosiers** – bottom. **Page 2: L.P. Wittman Limited** – top, bottom; **Shane Johnson Illustrations** – top left; **Shutterstock** – top right. **Page 3: Bridgeman Art Library** – top; **Shane Johnson Illustrations** – top right; **The Crosiers** – top left; **Shutterstock** – bottom. **Page 4: Shutterstock** – top, top right; **Shane Johnson Illustrations** – top left. **UNIT 1: Shane Johnson Illustrations** – pgs 15, 19, 35, 51, 67 (bottom); **Shutterstock**–pgs 17, 27, 28, 35, 41, 43, 49, 51, 59, 61, 69, 71 (bottom); **The Crosiers** – pgs 18, 19, 21, 29, 33, 34, 36, 38, 44, 46, 62, 63 (bottom), 70; **Catholic News Service** – pg 20, 37, 45, 52, 53; **Bridgeman Art Library** – pgs 22, 30, 36, 42, 50, 54, 57, 58, 60, 66, 68; **Design Pics** – pgs 23, 31, 39, 47, 65, 67 (top); **Jupiter Unlimited** – pgs 25, 71 (top); **The Granger Collection** pg 26; **L.P. Wittman Limited** – pg 55; **Jupiter** – pg 63 (top). **UNIT 2: Shane Johnson Illustrations** – pgs 75, 76, 87, 95, 103; **Jupiter Unlimited** – pgs 77, 91; **The Granger Collection** – pgs 78, 102; **Shutterstock** – pgs 79, 86, 97, 105, 107; **L.P. Wittman Limited** – pgs 80, 81, 82, 83 (top), 85, 88, 89, 93, 96, 101, 104; **The Crosiers** – pgs 83 (bottom), 90; **Bridgeman Art Library** – pgs 94, 106 (top); **Catholic News Service** – pg 98; **Design Pics** – pg 99; **OSV file image** – pg 106 (bottom). **UNIT 3: Shane Johnson Illustrations** – pgs 111, 123 (bottom), 139 (bottom), 155 (bottom); **Shutterstock** – pgs 112, 115 (top), 116, 121, 123 (top), 125, 127 (bottom), 137, 139 (top), 140, 141 (top), 147, 151 (bottom), 155 (top); **Jupiter Unlimited** – pgs 113, 127 (top), 143 (bottom), 145, 151 (top), 159; **The Crosiers** – pgs 114, 122, 126, 138, 150, 154; **Design Pics** – pgs 115, 131, 143 (top); **Catholic News Service** – pgs 118, 133; **L.P. Wittman Limited** – pgs 119, 129, 132, 135 (top), 141 (bottom), 156, 158; **The Granger Collection** – pg 124; **Bridgeman Art Library** – pgs 130, 146, 149; **OSV file image** – pg 117, 134; **Fran Gregory** – pg 142; **Sarah Hayes** – pg 153. **UNIT 4: Shane Johnson Illustrations** – pgs 163, 175 (bottom); **Shutterstock** – pgs 164, 171, 173, 177 (bottom), 182, 185; **Jupiter Unlimited** – pg 165; **The Crosiers** – pgs 166, 170, 175 (top), 181, 186, 187 (bottom) ;**L.P. Wittman Limited** – pgs 168, 176, 177 (top), 179, 183, 184, 187 (top); **The Granger Collection** – pg 169; **Bridgeman Art Library** – pg 174; **OSV file image** – pg 178. **RESOURCE SECTION: Shutterstock** – pgs 195 (top), 198 (top), 200 (bottom), 202, 206, 207, 212, 216; **Design Pics** – pgs 195 (bottom), 199 (bottom), 204 (top); **James Baca** – pg 197; **The Crosiers** – pg 198 (bottom), 200 (top), 201, 203, 219; **Shane Johnson Illustrations** – pgs 199 (top), 204 (bottom), 208 (top); **Jupiter Unlimited** – pgs 200 (left), 205; **L.P. Wittman Limited** – pgs 208 (bottom), 209, 213, 218; **Catholic News Service** – pgs 211, 214

Webcrafters, Inc.
Madison, WI, United States of America
November 2013
Job Number: 107406

Table of Contents

UNIT 1
The Profession of Faith

Being Catholic: Our Relationship with God Through the Sacraments 13

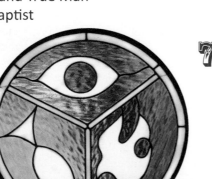

UNIT 2
Celebrating the Christian Mystery

UNIT 3
The Christian Life

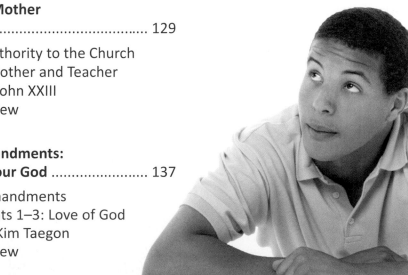

UNIT 4
Christian Prayer

Two-sided pullout poster features a timeline of Church history events from the birth of Jesus through the election of Pope Benedict XVI, placed in the context of world history events from the destruction of the Temple in Jerusalem to the election of the first African-American U.S. president.

FOREWORD

In reading *Faith Fusion* I kept saying to myself, "wholeness," a buzzword from psychology, but actually fulfilled in this user-friendly text. I commend the authors for designing a tapestry in true renaissance style instead of a narrow teaching tool. They seem to have forgotten nothing in thinking of ways to make Catholic teaching accessible and a relationship with Christ credible.

Here you will find Scripture, Tradition, liturgy, prayer, Church history, saints' lives, Catholic customs, and ethnic sensitivity presented in an integrated manner. Woven into these elements are recurrent forms of life applications: What does it mean to you? How does this make you a better Catholic? How does this help you to want the best for yourselves and others? Readers will have little chance to idly wonder over this or that aspect of a teaching.

Every lesson contains a story of a saint, a practice that dates in catechesis from the earliest days of the Church. The power of a personal witness story inspires and motivates the listener to act on the teaching that is illustrated—and is effectively used in this text.

Everyone profits from a "Catch-up" or review of the faith from time to time. This is especially true when one is in transition, such as during Confirmation preparation, participation in RCIA, and in high school youth ministry.

Clear, direct, and challenging, this text owns a simplicity that is admirable. Distilled wisdom always is. It was an excellent idea to use the *Compendium of the Catechism of the Catholic Church*. At the same time it was important to give prominence to Scripture, which is missing in the *Compendium*.

The authors wisely followed the sequence of the four pillars of the *Catechism of the Catholic Church*: Creed, Liturgy, Life in Christ, Prayer. These pillars lead the learner to ponder the faith believed, the faith celebrated, the faith in moral practice, and the faith prayed.

This approach invites the young people to hear the voice of the Father and see the face of Christ and live in the house of the Church with the Holy Spirit. It gives them a map of life for this earth and the goal of eternal life hereafter.

Rev. Alfred McBride, O.Praem.

We Answer God's Call

God of all faithfulness,
you have made us in your image and likeness.
You have called us by name
to be your disciples and to serve you.
You bless us with your love
in all the circumstances of our lives.
Send your Holy Spirit upon us
that we may be faithful to
our baptismal promises
and live and work together
for the glory of your name.
We ask this in the name of
Jesus Christ, our Lord.
Amen.

AN INTRODUCTION TO THE
Catechism of the Catholic Church

A catechism is a book containing the truths of the Faith, especially an explanation of the Creed, the liturgy and Sacraments, the Commandments, and prayer. A catechism is designed to help teach the faith, to clarify points of doctrine, and to provide guidance on how the faith should be lived.

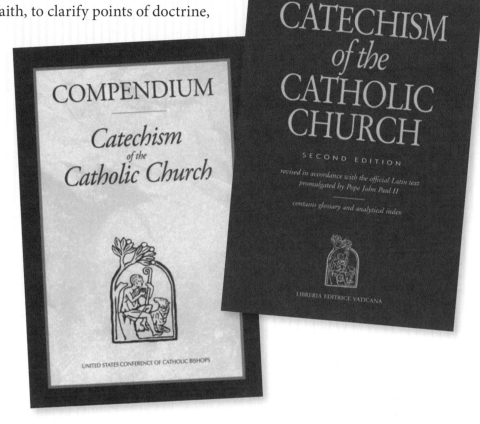

Over the centuries, many catechisms have been written, including the *Roman Catechism*, issued in 1566 by Pope Saint Pius V, and the *Baltimore Catechism*, produced in the United States near the end of the nineteenth century. In 1992, after six years of preparation, *The Catechism of the Catholic Church*, commissioned by Pope John Paul II, was published.

The *Catechism* presents and preserves the truths of our faith contained in Sacred Scripture and in the Church's Tradition, handed on since the time of the Apostles. It is from these sources that the Church draws all its teachings and presents them to the faithful as divinely revealed.

The foundation of the *Catechism* is Sacred Scripture, which has a preeminent place in the Church's teaching and life, because it is the authentic Word of God. The *Catechism* also includes the writings of the Fathers of the Church, such as Saint Jerome and Saint Augustine, and of doctors of the Church and saints.

Pope John Paul II described the *Catechism* as the "symphony" of the faith, because it is the result of the collaboration and contributions of the bishops of the Catholic Church from around the world, and because it expresses the harmony of their affirmation of the faith.

HOW TO USE THE CATECHISM

The *Catechism of the Catholic Church* is arranged in four parts, each corresponding to an essential aspect of the Christian mystery:

1. The Profession of the Faith. This section expresses the belief in the Blessed Trinity and God's plan for salvation as fulfilled in Jesus Christ.

2. The Celebration of the Christian Mystery. The People of God, the Church, celebrate Christ's work of salvation through the Church's liturgy and the Sacraments.

3. Life in Christ. Through the Scriptures and the Church, we learn how we are to live as followers of Christ.

4. Christian Prayer. Through personal and communal prayer, we express our faith in God and in all that he has made known to us.

The Celebration of the Christian Mystery 355

IN BRIEF

1406   Jesus said: "I am the living bread that came down from heaven; if any one eats of this bread, he will live for ever; . . . he who eats my flesh and drinks my blood has eternal life and . . . abides in me, and I in him" (Jn 6:51, 54, 56).

1407   The Eucharist is the heart and the summit of the Church's life, for in it Christ associates his Church and all her members with his sacrifice of praise and thanksgiving offered once for all on the cross to his Father; by this sacrifice he pours out the graces of salvation on his Body which is the Church.

1408   The Eucharistic celebration always includes: the proclamation of the Word of God; thanksgiving to God the Father for all his benefits, above all the gift of his Son; the consecration of bread and wine; and participation in the liturgical banquet by receiving the Lord's body and blood. These elements constitute one single act of worship.

1409   The Eucharist is the memorial of Christ's Passover, that is, of the work of salvation accomplished by the life, death, and resurrection of Christ, a work made present by the liturgical action.

1410   It is Christ himself, the eternal high priest of the New Covenant who, acting through the ministry of the priests, offers the Eucharistic sacrifice. And it is the same Christ, really present under the species of bread and wine, who is the offering of the Eucharistic sacrifice.

1411   Only validly ordained priests can preside at the Eucharist and consecrate the bread and the wine so that they become the Body and Blood of the Lord.

1412   The essential signs of the Eucharistic sacrament are wheat bread and grape wine, on which the blessing of the Holy Spirit is invoked and the priest pronounces the words of consecration spoken by Jesus during the Last Supper: "This is my body which will be given up for you. . . . This is the cup of my blood. . . ."

249   *LG* 3; St. Ignatius of Antioch, *Ad Eph.* 20, 2: SCh 10, 76.

PART TWO

THE CELEBRATION OF THE CHRISTIAN MYSTERY

Why the liturgy?

1066   In the Symbol of the faith the Church confesses the mystery of the Holy Trinity and of the plan of God's "good pleasure" for all creation: the Father accomplishes the "mystery of his will" by giving his beloved Son and his Holy Spirit for the salvation of the world and for the glory of his name.[1] Such is the mystery of Christ, revealed and fulfilled in history according to the wisely ordered plan that St. Paul calls the "plan of the mystery"[2] and the patristic tradition will call the "economy of the Word incarnate" or the "economy of salvation."

1067   "The wonderful works of God among the people of the Old Testament were but a prelude to the work of Christ the Lord in redeeming mankind and giving perfect glory to God. He accomplished this work principally by the Paschal mystery of his blessed Passion, Resurrection from the dead, and glorious Ascension, whereby 'dying he destroyed our death, rising he restored our life.' For it was from the side of Christ as he slept the sleep of death upon the cross that there came forth 'the wondrous sacrament of the whole Church.'"[3] For this reason, the Church celebrates in the liturgy above all the Paschal mystery by which Christ accomplished the work of our salvation.

1068   It is this mystery of Christ that the Church proclaims and celebrates in her liturgy so that the faithful may live from it and bear witness to it in the world:

50

236

571

1   *Eph* 1:9.
2   *Eph* 3:9; cf. 3:4.
3   SC 5 § 2; cf. St. Augustine, *En. in Ps.* 138, 2: PL 37, 1784-1785.

Each of the four parts is further divided into chapters dealing with specific issues. As you read, you will see that there are bold headings, which give an overview of the topic. Under those will be more detailed, explanatory information. In some instances, even more information will be presented in subheads. Each chapter ends with "In Brief," a summation of the key concepts of that section. As you read, you may find it helpful to read "In Brief" first to get an idea of what the section is about. Then go back and read the sections. Finally, ask God to reveal to you what it is that he wants you to know and understand about that section.

TEST YOUR FAITH IQ

How Much Do You Know About Your Catholic Faith?

Take the following quiz to see how well you know the teachings of your Catholic faith. Don't worry about your number of incorrect answers. Retake this quiz after completing this program and see how much more you know then.

1 The Our Father is also called "the Lord's Prayer" because _____.

a Jesus gave it that title

b Jesus is the author of the prayer

c it is the prayer Jesus prayed

d it is the most perfect of prayers

2 The central mystery of our Christian faith is the mystery of _____ .

a Scriptures

b the Holy Spirit

c the Blessed Trinity

d God the Son

3 Through the Sacraments of Christian Initiation we enter into full membership in the Church. These Sacraments are _____.

a Baptism, Penance, and Eucharist

b Baptism and Confirmation

c Confirmation and Eucharist

d Baptism, Eucharist, and Confirmation

4 The Marks of the Church that we profess in the Nicene Creed are that the Church is _____.

a Catholic, Universal, Holy, and Missionary

b One, Holy, Catholic, and Apostolic

c Holy, Catholic, Apostolic, and Sacred

d One, Catholic, Universal, and Holy

5 In the Scriptures God gradually made himself known to us through his words and deeds. This is called _____.

a faith

b Deposit of Faith

c Divine Revelation

d Tradition

6 The mystery of Jesus Christ, the divine Son of God, becoming man is called the _____.

a Incarnation

b Resurrection

c Nativity

d Ascension

7 During the Sermon on the Mount, Jesus taught _____ , in which he described the qualities those who are part of the Kingdom of God must have.

a the Beatitudes

b the Psalms

c the Epistles

d the Ten Commandments

8 Jesus promised his Apostles that after he ascended into Heaven he would send the Holy Spirit to guide them. The Holy Spirit descended upon the Apostles on _____.

a Easter

b Lent

c the Annunciation

d Pentecost

9 Which of the Sacraments did Jesus institute on the night before he died?

a Confirmation

b the Eucharist

c Baptism

d Matrimony

10 What is our internal ability to judge what is morally right or wrong called?

a ego

b moral compass

c human nature

d conscience

11 Which of the following is not an example of a devotion?

a praying the Stations of the Cross
b making a pilgrimage to the Holy Land
c receiving blessed ashes on Ash Wednesday
d attending the celebration of the Mass

12 God gives the freedom to choose between good and evil. This is called _____.

a free will
b virtue
c sanctifying grace
d the Story of the Fall

13 The first three Commandments guide our relationship with God, and the remaining seven guide _____.

a our interactions with other people
b our ability to choose a vocation
c the friendships we choose
d our observance of the Holy Days of Obligation

14 Mary was free from Original Sin from the moment she was conceived. This is known as _____.

a the Incarnation
b the Immaculate Conception
c Pentecost
d the Assumption

15 Which of the following is not a source of moral guidance for us?

a the Sermon on the Mount
b the Bill of Rights
c the Church's teachings
d the Ten Commandments

16 Heaven is _____.

a everlasting happiness with God and with all people who love him
b everlasting happiness with our loved ones
c a physical place
d a Mark of the Church

17 Among all his creation, God set us apart by _____.

a creating us in his likeness
b creating us on the seventh day
c giving us the Garden of Eden
d giving us the tree of knowledge

18 What is the first of the Ten Commandments?

a Remember to keep holy the Lord's Day.
b You shall not take the name of the Lord your God in vain.
c Honor your father and mother.
d I am the Lord your God: you shall not have strange gods before me.

19 When we pray we must _____.

a ask for things we need
b speak aloud
c talk and listen to God
d make the Sign of the Cross

20 Baptized men are ordained for permanent ministry in the Church as bishops, priests, or deacons in the Sacrament of _____.

a Eucharist
b Anointing of the Sick
c Holy Orders
d Matrimony

Your Score Now _____

Your Year-end Score _____

Being Catholic

OUR RELATIONSHIP WITH GOD THROUGH THE SACRAMENTS

WHAT'S IN A NAME?

People choose Confirmation names for many reasons. Most select the name in honor of a saint, or perhaps they select a particular saint's name because of a special relative or friend whom they admire. Others select the name just because they like it. Some decide to keep their baptismal name, if it's the name of a saint. Whatever the reason for your choice, be sure that you learn more about the saint, and to ask him or her to help you in living out your Christian faith.

Which saint's name are you thinking about choosing or have you already selected for Confirmation? Why did you select this saint's name?

> "I have called you friends because I have told you everything I have heard from my father."
> —John 15:15

BELIEF IN GOD—IT'S MORE THAN AN OBLIGATION

How strongly do you feel about your faith? Do you practice your faith merely out of obligation? Many of the saints in our Church died for their faith. People who die in the name of the Church are known as martyrs. Do you think the martyrs gave up their life for believing in Jesus Christ because they were told to, or because they felt obligated?

It's easy to think about religion or believing in God as something we have to do. Come to class, study prayers and teachings, fill out forms—the list can go on. But completing all of these requirements does not make us Catholic. What we believe in our hearts about God, Jesus Christ, the Holy Spirit, and the Church, and living according to those beliefs, is what makes us true believers. Like the saints, we are called to willingly live out our faith and to grow in our relationship with God.

What challenges do you face in living out your faith? In what ways do you live out your faith in your daily life?

BUILDING A RELATIONSHIP WITH GOD

At the Last Supper, Jesus said to his disciples, "I call you friends because I have told you everything I have heard from my Father" (John 15:15). He did not just command his disciples to follow certain rules; he spoke to them of friendship. In the same way, Jesus calls us to a friendship with himself and with God. And just as we would strive to strengthen important friendships in our lives, we must work to build our relationship with God, looking upon it as a warm and loving friendship that enriches our minds, hearts, and souls. Of course, our relationship with God does require that we follow certain rules—the Commandments, the Church's teachings, and what the Scriptures tell us. Following these rules builds the foundation for a loving relationship with God.

In an address to youth and seminarians during his visit to the United States in 2008, Pope Benedict XVI said that we can enter into this relationship with God by living out our faith in the following ways:

- Personal prayer and silence
- Liturgical prayer
- Charity in action
- Our vocation

In all we say and do, it is important that we allow Jesus to enter into our lives. This is our mission in being faithful Catholics and followers of Jesus Christ.

What does my faith mean to me? What more can I do to make my relationship with God stronger?

Believing

UNIT 1

The Profession of Faith

The one true God, our Creator and Lord,
can be known with certainty from his works,
by the natural light of human reason. (CCC, 47)

The Nicene Creed

I believe in one God,
the Father almighty,
maker of heaven and earth,
of all things visible and invisible.
I believe in one Lord Jesus Christ,
the Only Begotten Son of God,
born of the Father before all ages.
God from God, Light from Light,
true God from true God,
begotten, not made,
consubstantial with the Father;
through him all things were made.
For us men and for our salvation
he came down from heaven,
and by the Holy Spirit was incarnate
of the Virgin Mary,
and became man.
For our sake he was crucified
under Pontius Pilate,
he suffered death and was buried,
and rose again on the third day
in accordance with the Scriptures.
He ascended into heaven
and is seated at the right hand of the Father.
He will come again in glory
to judge the living and the dead
and his kingdom will have no end.
I believe in the Holy Spirit, the Lord,
the giver of life,
who proceeds from the Father and the Son,
who with the Father and the Son
is adored and glorified,
who has spoken through the prophets.
I believe in one, holy,
catholic and apostolic Church.
I confess one baptism for the forgiveness of sins
and I look forward to
the resurrection of the dead
and the life of the world to come.
Amen.

The Revelation of God and Sacred Scripture

A Psalm Prayer

I will extol you, my God and king;
  I will bless your name forever.
Every day I will bless you;
  I will praise your name forever.
Great is the LORD and worthy of high praise;
  God's grandeur is beyond understanding.

—Psalm 145:1–3

Live It Out

God leads us to himself through the Scriptures and the Church. Reflect on ways that the Bible and your Catholic faith affect the way you live your life. What are some specific times when they have guided you?

BIBLE BOOST

> *Proclaim the word; be persistent whether it is convenient or inconvenient.*

The Guidance of the Scriptures

The following Scripture passage comes from the second **epistle**, or letter, of Saint Paul to Timothy, the leader of the Christian community in Ephesus. In this letter, Paul urges Timothy to protect the community he leads from the false teachings of others. He recommends that Timothy rely on the power of the Scriptures and on sound teaching to lead his congregation.

SACRED SCRIPTURE

A READING FROM THE SECOND LETTER OF PAUL TO TIMOTHY

Remain faithful to what you have learned and believed, because you know from whom you learned it, and that from infancy you have known [the] sacred scriptures, which are capable of giving you wisdom for salvation through faith in Christ Jesus. All scripture is inspired by God and is useful for teaching, for refutation, for correction, and for training in righteousness, so that one who belongs to God may be competent, equipped for every good work.

I charge you in the presence of God and of Christ Jesus, who will judge the living and the dead, and by his appearing and his kingly power: proclaim the word; be persistent whether it is convenient or inconvenient; convince, reprimand, encourage through all patience and teaching.

—2 Timothy 3:14—4:2

START LIVING

In his letter to Timothy, Saint Paul tells him how he should lead the Christians in his community. Imagine that you are receiving instructions about how you should lead others in the Christian faith, either by your words or your example.

Describe two specific actions you might be instructed to take.

Giving advice to friends, going to church, being kind to every one

What are some ways you might follow Saint Paul's instruction to proclaim the Gospel even when it is inconvenient?

respecting others reading the bible

During the Mass
This Scripture passage from 2 Timothy is the Second Reading at Mass on the Twenty-ninth Sunday in Ordinary Time, during Year C. See pages 218–219.

KNOW IT!

epistle
a letter found in the New Testament, written to the early Christian communities or those who led them

OUR CATHOLIC TRADITION

Make every effort to supplement your faith with virtue.
—2 Peter 1:5

Sacred Scripture and Tradition

When the Founding Fathers wrote the U.S. Constitution more than 230 years ago, they left us with a record of the rules we are to follow as members of American society. Ever since its writing, however, generations of scholars have strived to interpret what the words of the Constitution mean, especially for the people of their time, so it can guide American society and shape its laws.

It is the same with Scriptures and our Catholic faith. God is the author of Sacred Scripture because he inspired its human authors. Throughout the Scriptures, in the Old Testament and the New Testament, God gradually reveals to us in words and deeds his great love for us and his plan for our salvation. From the beginning, through the events of Creation, God made known to us the mystery of who he is. He continued his revelation through his relationship with the Israelites, in leading them out of slavery in Egypt. The culmination of God's self-revelation is made in the person of his Son, Jesus Christ, through whom God's plan for our salvation is fulfilled. God's making himself known is called **Divine Revelation**.

The truth of who God is as revealed in the Scriptures must be interpreted throughout time, so that its message of salvation can be applied to our lives today. Through **Tradition**, made visible in the Church's teachings, life, and worship, with the guidance of the Holy Spirit, the Church passes on to all generations the meaning of God's revelation and the way the faithful are to live it. The Church's Tradition includes all that Christ entrusted to the Church through the Apostles, which they handed down by their preaching, writings, and worship. Together, Sacred Scripture and Tradition make up one sacred **Deposit of Faith** of the Word of God. The task of interpreting the Deposit of Faith has been entrusted to the living teaching office of the Church, the **Magisterium**, made up of the Pope and all the bishops. With the guidance of the Holy Spirit, the Magisterium interprets Scripture and Tradition, and teaches us how to apply their message to our lives.

It is part of human nature to search and long for God. Yet God remains a mystery beyond words for us. So great is God's gift of himself and love for us that it is only through **faith** that we can be open to it. Faith is a gift of God's grace that enables us to believe. It is strengthened by the help of the Holy Spirit and nourished by the Church. Our faith in God leads us to turn to him alone as our Creator, and to put him above all else in our lives.

CATECHISM Q&A

Q. What makes up the Scriptures?

A. The Bible is composed of the forty-six books of the Old Testament and the twenty-seven books of the New Testament. Together these make up the Scriptures that the Church accepts and venerates as inspired by the Holy Spirit. (See *Compendium*, Question 20; *CCC*, 120.)

Q. Why do the Gospels hold a special place of honor among all the books of the Bible?

A. The four Gospels, the Books of Matthew, Mark, Luke, and John, occupy a central place in all Scripture because they tell us about Jesus Christ and contain his teachings. (See *Compendium*, Question 22; *CCC*, 127.)

CATHOLIC CUSTOMS
PILGRIMAGE

A pilgrimage is a journey to a shrine or holy site to pray for special blessings. The Christian practice of making pilgrimages began in the fourth century, with the Holy Land one of the most important pilgrimage sites. Popular pilgrimage sites for Catholics today include the Shrine of Our Lady of Lourdes in France and the Basilica of Our Lady of Guadalupe in Mexico.

KNOW and BELIEVE

Who in your life has been especially important in helping you learn about your Catholic faith? Describe one way that you can share with others what you believe as a Catholic.

My brother has helped me learn about the catholic faith. God is more important than anything.

KNOW iT!

Divine Revelation
God's gift of making himself known to us and giving himself to us by gradually communicating his own mystery in words and deeds

Tradition
the transmission of the message of the Gospel as lived out by the Church, past and present

faith
a gift from God that enables us to believe in him and all that he has revealed

SAINTLY *profiles*

Throughout the Church's history, many people have contributed to our understanding of our Catholic faith. The Church honors those who made exceptional contributions to the Church's learning with the title "**Doctor of the Church**."

Saint Jerome 342–420

Saint Jerome was born in the Roman province of Dalmatia. As a young man, he was sent by his father to Rome to study. There he became fluent in Latin and Greek. Jerome avidly read the literature of those languages and acquired many worldly ideas. In spite of these influences, Jerome was baptized into the Christian faith in 360.

After three years in Rome, Jerome left to explore other parts of the world. It was during these travels that he dedicated himself fully to God. As a way to grow in his faith, Jerome chose to move to a desert near Antioch, where he could live in solitude as a hermit. During this time, Jerome worked on a number of important writings, many explaining the Church's beliefs and teachings. His greatest work, however, was his translation of the Bible from Hebrew and Greek into Latin, the language of the people of the Western Roman Empire. Jerome completed this translation, which became known as the **Vulgate**, in 405. It is still the Church's official translation of the Bible.

Because of Jerome's great contribution to the Church's teachings, especially his study and translation of the Scriptures, the Church declared him a saint and a Doctor of the Church.

ALL ABOUT
SAINT JEROME

✳ Worked on the Vulgate for about fifteen years

✳ According to legend, he once drew a thorn from the paw of a lion

✳ In artwork, he is frequently depicted in the desert, as a scholar, in cardinal's attire (because of his service to Pope Damasus), and with a lion

✳ Died in 420, in Bethlehem

FEAST DAY: September 30
PATRONAGE: Scripture scholars, translators, librarians

MAKE IT HAPPEN

Saint Jerome dedicated himself to God and sought to serve him by studying and translating the Scriptures. Consider the following quote from Scripture and explain what its message for you might be.

> "Your light must shine before others, that they may see your good deeds and glorify your heavenly Father."
>
> —Matthew 5:16

You should show off your special interests and talents so others can see.

Catholic Social Teaching
SOLIDARITY

Solidarity is a Christian virtue that calls for the sharing of spiritual goods as well as material ones. Because every human life is created in the image and likeness of God, the Church teaches that we are all part of one human family and that we are all responsible for one another. By living according to this teaching, we follow Jesus' command to love our neighbor as ourselves.

Choose one way that you can put this teaching into practice this week.

LET US PRAY

A Prayer for Openness to God's Word
Your word, LORD, stands forever;
* it is firm as the heavens.*
Through all generations your truth endures;
* fixed to stand firm like the earth.*
Your word is a lamp for my feet,
* a light for my path.*

—Psalm 119:89–90, 105

KNOW IT!

Doctor of the Church
a title given by the Church to those whose writings have helped others understand faith or doctrine

Vulgate
the version of the Bible translated from Hebrew and Greek into Latin by Saint Jerome in the early fifth century

YOUR TURN

A. Circle the letter of the correct answer.

1 God's gift of making himself known to us by gradually communicating his own mystery in words and deeds is called ___A___ . *(3) P*

- **a** Divine Revelation
- **b** Deposit of Faith
- **c** faith
- **d** Tradition

2 Saint Jerome's translation of the Bible from Hebrew and Greek into Latin is known as the ___C___ . *(23) P*

- **a** Epistles
- **b** Deposit of Faith
- **c** Vulgate
- **d** Old Testament

3 ___B___ is a gift from God that enables us to believe in him and all that he has revealed. *(21) P*

- **a** The Church
- **b** Faith
- **c** Sacred Scripture
- **d** The Deposit of Faith

4 The transmission of the message of the Gospel as lived out by the Church, past and present, is called ___A___ . *(21) P*

- **a** Tradition
- **b** Sacred Scripture
- **c** a pilgrimage
- **d** the Gospels

5 ___C___ is a title given by the Church to those whose writings have helped others understand faith or doctrine. *(23) P*

- **a** Deposit of Faith
- **b** saint
- **c** Doctor of the Church
- **d** Magisterium

6 An epistle is ___b___ . *(19) P*

- **a** the combination of Scripture and Tradition
- **b** a New Testament letter written to the early Christian communities or those who led them
- **c** any of the books of the Old Testament
- **d** the belief that we are all part of one human family

B. Respond to the following. *20*

In what ways has God revealed himself to us throughout time?

By words and deads, scriptures.

How might a deeper knowledge of the Scriptures help you know more about God's Revelation?

I Believe in God the Father

A Prayer of Praise

O LORD, our Lord,
   how awesome is your name above all the earth!
   You have set your majesty above the heavens!
   What are humans that you are mindful of them,
   mere mortals that you should care for them?

—Psalm 8:2, 5

Live It Out

God is our loving Father who looks after all our needs. How does a loving father care for his children? How do you live your life in a way that welcomes God as your loving Father?

BIBLE BOOST

> *If you love me, you will keep my commandments. And I will ask the Father, and he will give you another Advocate to be with you always.*

The Father Sends the Holy Spirit

Throughout the Gospels, Jesus makes repeated references to God the Father, who calls us to share in eternal glory with him. In the following Scripture reading, Jesus tells his disciples that he will ask the Father to send the Holy Spirit to those who believe in him.

Trinity, Andrei Rublev, 1411 (tempera on panel, Moscow)

SACRED SCRIPTURE

A READING FROM THE HOLY GOSPEL ACCORDING TO JOHN

"If you love me, you will keep my commandments. And I will ask the Father, and he will give you another Advocate to be with you always. Whoever loves me will keep my word, and my Father will love him, and we will come to him and make our dwelling with him. Whoever does not love me does not keep my words; yet the word you hear is not mine but that of the Father who sent me.

"I have told you this while I am with you. The Advocate, the holy Spirit that the Father will send in my name—he will teach you everything and remind you of all that I told you."

—John 14:15–16, 23–26

START LIVING

When Jesus speaks to his disciples about the relationship they are to have with him and with God the Father, he tells them that God will be with those who follow his commandments and will provide to them all the help they need.

Describe one way that you try to live according to God's commandments, and one way that God helps you to do so.

The guidance that God gives us to live according to his commandments often comes through people in our lives. **Identify two people in your life who help you live as a follower of Jesus and at least one way that you can be more open to guidance from these people.**

Person who helps me follow Jesus	Ways I can be more open to this person's guidance

Stop and Think

Choose a phrase from the Scripture reading that can guide you in how you live your life. What is its message for you?

As the deer longs for streams of water, so my soul longs for you, O God.
—Psalm 42:2

Creation of Adam, Michelangelo Buonarroti, c. 1510 (fresco, Sistine Chapel, Vatican City)

God, Our Loving Father

In the Old Testament, God gradually revealed himself to his people in deeds and in words, and through the **covenants** he made with our first parents, with Noah, and with Abraham and his descendants. In the New Testament we learn that it is in Jesus, his only Son, that God the Father establishes his covenant forever.

Through Noah, Abraham, and the law God gave to his people through Moses, the Jews of the Old Testament had come to believe in the one true God. But Jesus taught his followers more about God: that he is a loving Father, who looks after all our needs. Jesus also promised us that God would send the Holy Spirit to guide us to himself. The Holy Spirit guides the Church to do the work of Christ. God the Father, God the Son, and God the Holy Spirit are Three Divine Persons in one God, the **Blessed Trinity**.

God the Father is the First Person of the Blessed Trinity. He is our loving Creator. He alone is the Creator of the universe, which he created freely and of his own will. Although the work of Creation is attributed to God the Father, the Father, Son, and Holy Spirit are one, and are together the source of all Creation. God's love for us is everlasting, and was first shown to us when he created the world. He created us that we may live in communion with him, and he created the universe out of love for us, so that we may share in his goodness and glory.

As Catholics, we believe in one true God in Three Divine Persons. Although this mystery of the Blessed Trinity is beyond our ability to understand, it is the central mystery of our Christian faith.

CATECHISM Q&A

Q. Which of the three Persons of the Blessed Trinity is recognized as the Creator?

A. God the Father is recognized as the Creator, yet the Father, Son, and Holy Spirit are one and indivisible, and are together the source of Creation. (See *Compendium*, Question 52; *CCC*, 316.)

Q. What is the central mystery of our Christian faith?

A. The central mystery of our faith is the mystery of the Most Holy Trinity, one God in Three Divine Persons, Father, Son, and Holy Spirit. (See *Compendium*, Question 44; *CCC*, 261.)

COMPENDIUM
Catechism of the Catholic Church

CATECHISM *of the* CATHOLIC CHURCH
SECOND EDITION
revised in accordance with the official Latin text promulgated by Pope John Paul II
contains glossary and analytical index

Calendar Connection
The Nicene Creed

WHO The Fathers of the Church

WHAT The Nicene Creed, which expresses our belief in one God: God the Father, God the Son, and God the Holy Spirit. We pray the Nicene Creed at Mass every Sunday.

WHERE Nicea, in modern-day Turkey

WHEN A.D. 325, at the Council of Nicea, and at the following three Church councils

WHY To develop a way of describing the mystery of the Trinity

KNOW and BELIEVE

God is our loving Father. He has a special love for every person, and a special plan for each of us. In what ways can you be more accepting of God's plan for you and more open to following his will?

_____

_____

_____

_____

_____

_____

KNOW IT!

covenant
in Scriptures, a sacred agreement between God and his people

Blessed Trinity
the one God in Three Divine Persons: God the Father, God the Son, and God the Holy Spirit

SAINTLY *profiles*

The mystery of the Blessed Trinity is beyond our human understanding. However, Saint Thomas Aquinas, one of the Church's greatest thinkers, showed that through human reason we can grow in our knowledge of God and in our faith.

Saint Thomas Aquinas 1225–1274

Thomas Aquinas was born to a noble Italian family. At the age of five his family placed him in the care of the Benedictine monks at the monastery in Monte Cassino. Thomas showed exceptional intelligence from an early age, often asking his teachers, "Who is God?" When he was seventeen, Thomas joined the Dominican order of religious, despite his family's opposition. With the Dominicans, he began his studies at the University of Paris, where he studied theology and philosophy and later was a teacher.

Thomas Aquinas was a brilliant scholar, and his writings are a great contribution to our understanding about God. He viewed theology, or the study of God, as a science, drawn from the Scriptures and Church Tradition, and believed that both faith and logic were necessary for knowing God. In his greatest work, the *Summa Theologiae*, he wrote that God is eternal and is the cause of everything in the universe, and that through human reason, he can be known with certainty from his works.

Aquinas's writings also help us understand the Blessed Trinity. He wrote that God is perfectly described by the Three Persons of the Trinity, where the Father sends the Son, who together with the Father generates an eternal Spirit—the Holy Spirit.

ALL ABOUT
SAINT THOMAS AQUINAS

- ❋ One of the great teachers of the Catholic Church
- ❋ Asked by Pope Gregory X to participate in the Council of Lyon (1271–1276), but died on his way there
- ❋ Depicted in art holding a book or a church with rays of light emanating from his chest
- ❋ Symbols: Chalice, dove, and ox (because as a young student he was nicknamed "dumb ox"!)
- ❋ Canonized in 1323
- ❋ Named a Doctor of the Church in 1567

FEAST DAY: January 28
PATRONAGE: Catholic education

MAKE IT HAPPEN

Saint Thomas Aquinas made a great contribution to the Church by his brilliant writings, especially the *Summa Theologiae*, which showed that belief in God can be supported by faith and reason. In our own way, each of us is called to work to build up the Church.

Describe two ways in which you can build up the Church by helping others grow in their faith.

_____

_____

_____

_____

_____

KNOW iT!

Triqueta

This is an early Christian symbol of the Blessed Trinity. The interwoven continuity of the symbol represents the unity of the Three Persons of the Trinity—Father, Son, and Holy Spirit—and its arc of equal length signify their equality.

LET US PRAY

The Act of Faith

O my God, I firmly believe that you are one God in Three Divine Persons, Father, Son, and Holy Spirit. I believe that your Divine Son became man and died for our sins, and that he will come to judge the living and the dead. I believe these and all the truths which the Holy Catholic Church teaches, because you have revealed them, who are eternal truth and wisdom, who can neither deceive nor be deceived. In this faith I intend to live and die. Amen.

YOUR TURN

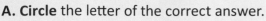

LESSON 2

A. Circle the letter of the correct answer.

1 The mystery of _____ is the central mystery of our Christian faith.

a Scriptures
b the Holy Spirit
c the Blessed Trinity
d the Nicene Creed

2 In his greatest work, the *Summa Theologiae*, Saint _____ wrote that God is eternal, and that his existence can be proved by human reason.

a Thomas More
b Jerome
c Ignatius
d Thomas Aquinas

3 Jesus taught us that God _____ .

a is the Second Person of the Blessed Trinity
b loves us only when we obey him
c is only the God of the Jews
d is a loving Father

4 A(n) _____ is a sacred agreement between God and his people.

a oath
b covenant
c creed
d ceremony

5 The creed we recite at Mass each Sunday is called the _____ .

a Nicene Creed
b Apostles' Creed
c *Summa Theologiae*
d Lord's Prayer

6 In the _____ , God gradually revealed himself to his people in words and in deeds.

a Old Testament
b New Testament
c *Summa Theologiae*
d Gospels

B. Respond to the following.

How did God the Father show his love for us through Creation?

_____

_____

_____

In what ways can you respond to God's love for you?

_____

_____

_____

A Believe in Jesus Christ, the Only Son of God

A Blessing Prayer

Blessed be the Lord,
    the God of Israel;
he has come to his people
    and set them free.
He has raised up
    for us a mighty savior,
born of the house of David.

—Based on Luke 1:68–69

Live It Out

When Mary accepted God's call to be the Mother of the Savior, she showed complete surrender to God's will. How can you develop a habit of being more open to God's plan for you?

33

BIBLE BOOST

> "Behold, the virgin shall be with child and bear a son, and they shall name him Emmanuel."

The Birth of Jesus

The Old Testament **prophet** Isaiah had told the Israelites that God would send a savior named Emmanuel. (See Isaiah 7:14.) By the power of the Holy Spirit, this promise was fulfilled in the birth of Jesus, through the cooperation of the Virgin Mary and Joseph.

SACRED SCRIPTURE

A READING FROM THE HOLY GOSPEL ACCORDING TO MATTHEW

This is how the birth of Jesus Christ came about. When his mother Mary was betrothed to Joseph, but before they lived together, she was found with child through the holy Spirit. Joseph her husband, since he was a righteous man, yet unwilling to expose her to shame, decided to divorce her quietly. Such was his intention when, behold, the angel of the Lord appeared to him in a dream and said, "Joseph, son of David, do not be afraid to take Mary your wife into your home. For it is through the holy Spirit that this child has been conceived in her. She will bear a son and you are to name him Jesus, because he will save his people from their sins." All this took place to fulfill what the Lord had said through the prophet:

> *"Behold, the virgin shall be with child and bear a son,*
> *and they shall name him Emmanuel,"*

which means "God is with us." When Joseph awoke, he did as the angel of the Lord had commanded him and took his wife into his home.

—Matthew 1:18–24

START LIVING

The Scripture passage from Matthew's Gospel recounts how the angel announced to Joseph that Mary would give birth to Jesus. At first Joseph was afraid of what this news meant for him and wanted to avoid the complications it would cause. Joseph then chose to accept God's will and to be Mary's husband and Jesus' foster father.

How can Joseph's response to God's will be an example for you when you are uncertain about how to respond to God?

_____
_____
_____
_____
_____

Describe a time in your life when at first God's plan for you was difficult to accept but then turned out to be for the best. Then describe what this experience can teach you about accepting God's will.

_____
_____
_____
_____
_____
_____

During the Mass
This Scripture passage from the Gospel of Matthew is read at Mass on the Fourth Sunday of Advent, during Year A. See pages 218–219.

KNOW IT!

prophet
a person whom God has chosen to speak in his name

OUR CATHOLIC TRADITION

Jesus: True God and True Man

Think about a time when someone told you he or she had good news for you. Perhaps it was news that an important math or English test that you were not prepared for had been postponed, or that a special relative was coming to visit. How did the news make you feel?

As Christians, we often hear about the Good News of salvation. This is similar to any other good news we might speak of and experience, but on a far grander scale, because it is the Good News of the **Incarnation**, the Son of God becoming man.

In the Old Testament, Isaiah spoke of the birth of a savior named Emmanuel, a name that means "God with us." Through the work of the Holy Spirit, the prophecy of Isaiah was fulfilled when Jesus, whose name means "God saves," was born of the Virgin Mary. Jesus is the Second Person of the Blessed Trinity. He is the only Son of the Father and is also God himself. He is truly God and truly man, and because of this he is the mediator between us and God.

During his life on earth, all Jesus said and did—his teachings, his miracles, his suffering—fulfilled God's revelation of who he is. Through Christ's earthly life, and especially through the **Paschal Mystery**—his human suffering and death and his Resurrection and **Ascension**—we have been redeemed and can have everlasting life with God. At the Ascension, Jesus returned to his Father in Heaven. From there he will come again in glory for the Last Judgment, when all people will be judged for how well they have lived and receive their eternal reward or eternal punishment.

CATECHISM Q&A

Q. Why is Jesus called Christ?

A. The word *Christ* comes from *Christos*, the Greek translation of the word **Messiah**, Hebrew for "anointed one." Jesus is the Messiah whom God sent for our salvation. (See *Compendium*, Question 82; *CCC*, 453.)

Q. What does the Ascension mean?

A. For forty days after his Resurrection, Jesus lived among the Apostles as man. He then ascended into Heaven, where he reigns with the Father and intercedes for us before the Father. (See *Compendium*, Question 132; *CCC*, 665, 667.)

CATHOLIC CUSTOMS
RELICS

A relic is a personal item or an object associated with Jesus or a saint or holy person. First-class relics are items directly associated with the events of Christ's life, such as pieces of the True Cross, or the physical remains of a saint, such as bone fragments. A second-class relic is an item that a saint or martyr wore or owned, such as a fragment of clothing or a prayer book. The Catholic Church venerates relics as a way to draw closer to Christ.

KNOW and BELIEVE

In all of his life, Jesus was a perfect model of discipleship for us, accepting God's will in all things. Write a prayer asking Jesus to help you follow his example of obedience to God and trust in his will for you.

_____

_____

_____

_____

_____

KNOW IT!

Incarnation
the mystery of Jesus Christ, the divine Son of God, becoming man

Paschal Mystery
the suffering, death, Resurrection, and Ascension of Jesus Christ

Ascension
Jesus' return in all his glory to his Father in Heaven

SAINTLY *profiles*

In Luke's Gospel we read about the Virgin Mary, carrying Jesus in her womb, visiting her cousin Elizabeth, who was also with child. When the two met, the child in Elizabeth's womb leapt with joy. This child was John the Baptist. This Gospel story reveals that even before his birth, John recognized the greatness of Jesus.

Saint John the Baptist d. first century

John the Baptist is the New Testament prophet who proclaimed the coming of Jesus, the Messiah, and reminded people of the need to prepare for his coming. John lived in the desert of Judea and attracted many followers. To all who would hear him he preached that to prepare for Jesus' coming, people needed to change the way they lived. He proclaimed, "Repent, for the kingdom of God is at hand" (Matthew 3:2). Many people came to John to be baptized, but some questioned his right to baptize, claiming that only the messiah could baptize. In reply John told them about Jesus, "I am baptizing you with water, for repentance, but the one who is coming after me is mightier than I. I am not worthy to carry his sandals. He will baptize you with the holy Spirit" (Matthew 3:11). John summed up his role in relation to Jesus when he said, "He must increase; I must decrease" (John 3:30). John knew that his importance was in leading others to Christ, in honoring him and bringing him the glory that he deserves.

Throughout his life John was fearless in criticizing sinful behavior and calling others to repent. It was this courage to speak out that led to his death. Fearful of his influence, King Herod Antipas had John imprisoned when he condemned Herod's sinful marriage to Herodias. Herodias and her daughter Salome sought revenge against John by asking the king for his head. King Herod doubted the justness of this punishment, yet he complied and had John the Baptist beheaded.

ALL ABOUT
SAINT JOHN THE BAPTIST

- Son of Elizabeth and Zechariah and a relative of Jesus
- Isaiah, the Old Testament prophet, foretold of John the Baptist as "the voice of one crying out in the desert, 'Prepare the way of the Lord, make straight his paths' " (see John 1:23)
- Presented in the New Testament as the last of the Old Testament prophets
- In liturgical art, often depicted carrying a staff that ends in a cross or holding his own head

FEAST DAYS: June 24 (birth), August 29 (martyrdom)

MAKE IT HAPPEN

John the Baptist lived in the desert and fully dedicated himself to bringing others to God. He lost his life when he criticized immoral behavior. We are not all called to show our commitment to our faith in such dramatic ways, but we are all called to lead others to God.

Give an example of a situation that you might face with your friends when you may need courage to speak against a wrong choice. How can John's words "Christ must increase; I must decrease" guide you in this situation?

_____

_____

_____

_____

_____

Catholic Social Teaching
LIFE AND DIGNITY OF THE HUMAN PERSON

The Catholic Church teaches that each person is created in God's image and that all people, including ourselves, have rights that flow from their human dignity. The equal dignity of all people means we must work to eliminate social and economic inequalities. As Catholics, we strive to value all people over our personal wealth or possessions.

How can you live out this teaching in your own life?

LET US PRAY

A Solemn Blessing
May the peace of God,
which surpasses all
  understanding,
keep your hearts and minds
in the knowledge and love
  of God,
and of his Son,
our Lord Jesus Christ.
—Solemn Blessing for Ordinary
  Time II, Roman Missal

YOUR TURN

A. Complete the following sentences, using words from the box.

1 A _____ is a person whom God has chosen to speak in his name.

2 Through the work of the _____, the prophecy of Isaiah was fulfilled when Jesus was born of the Virgin Mary.

3 The Paschal Mystery refers to the suffering, death, _____, and Ascension of Jesus Christ.

4 The _____ is the mystery of Jesus Christ, the divine Son of God, becoming man.

5 The word *Christ* comes from the Greek translation of the word _____, which means "Anointed One."

6 The _____ is Jesus Christ's return in glory to his Father in Heaven.

Incarnation
Holy Spirit
Ascension
Resurrection
prophet
Messiah

B. Respond to the following.

In what ways was John the Baptist a prophet?

_____

_____

_____

How can you be a prophet in the world today?

_____

_____

_____

_____

I Believe in the Holy Spirit

A Pentecost Prayer

Side 1: I saw the Lord ever before me,
with him at my right hand I shall not be
disturbed.

Side 2: [M]y heart has been glad and
my tongue has exulted;…
because you will not abandon
my soul to the netherworld,…

All: You have made known to me the paths of life;
you will fill me with joy in your presence.

—Acts 2:25–28

Live It Out

Have you ever been
challenged or criticized for
your faith? How did you
respond? How can the Holy
Spirit help you when you face
such challenges?

BIBLE BOOST

> *And suddenly there came from the sky a noise like a strong driving wind.*

The Coming of the Holy Spirit

At the time of Jesus' Ascension into Heaven, he spoke a final time to the Apostles, reassuring them that he would not abandon them. He promised them that they would receive the power of the Holy Spirit and that it would make them his witnesses to the end of the earth. (See Acts 1:8–9.) In the following Scripture passage, we read about the descent of the Holy Spirit upon the Apostles at **Pentecost**, in fulfillment of Christ's promise.

SACRED SCRIPTURE

A READING FROM THE ACTS OF THE APOSTLES

When the time for Pentecost was fulfilled, they were all in one place together. And, suddenly there came from the sky a noise like a strong driving wind, and it filled the entire house in which they were. Then there appeared to them tongues as of fire, which parted and came to rest on each of them. And they were all filled with the holy Spirit and began to speak in different tongues, as the Spirit enabled them to proclaim.

Now there were devout Jews from every nation under heaven staying in Jerusalem. At this sound, they gathered in a large crowd, but they were confused because each one heard them speaking in his own language. They were astounded, and in amazement they asked, "Are not all these people who are speaking Galileans? Then how does each of us hear them in his own native language? We are Parthians, Medes, Elamites, inhabitants of Mesopotamia, Judea and Cappadocia, Pontus and Asia, Phrygia and Pamphylia, Egypt and the districts of Libya near Cyrene, as well as travelers from Rome, both Jews and converts to Judaism, Cretans and Arabs, yet we hear them speaking in our own tongues of the mighty acts of God."

—Acts 2:1–11

START LIVING

When the Apostles received the Holy Spirit they were able to speak to the crowds gathered about God and be understood by all people. It is not always easy to speak to others about our faith with confidence.

How can the Holy Spirit help you when you need to speak about your faith?

_____
_____
_____

_____

When you are called upon to stand up for your faith, how might the Holy Spirit work in others to allow them to be more open to your words?

_____
_____
_____
_____

_____
_____
_____

Stop and Think

Choose a phrase from the Scripture reading that creates a vivid image of the Holy Spirit for you. What feelings does this phrase and its imagery give you?

_____
_____
_____

KNow iT!

Pentecost
the day on which the Holy Spirit came to Jesus' disciples, with Mary present among them; Pentecost marks the birth of the Church

OUR CATHOLIC TRADITION

> "I will ask the Father and he will give you another Advocate to be with you always."
> —John 14:16

The Holy Spirit Shares in Jesus' Mission

Throughout the Scriptures, the Holy Spirit plays an important role in God's work of creation and salvation. In the Book of Genesis, the Story of Creation speaks of a mighty wind that swept over the waters. (See Genesis 1:2.) The Holy Spirit also appears in the story of the Israelites' exodus out of Egypt, when God guided them through the desert with a column of clouds and a column of fire. (See Exodus 13:21.) Other references to the Holy Spirit in the Old Testament are associated with the prophets, who deliver God's message when the "spirit of God" comes upon them. (See, for example, 2 Chronicles 15:1.)

The Holy Spirit's greatest participation in God's work of salvation can be witnessed in the New Testament, beginning with the Incarnation, when by the power of the Holy Spirit, Mary conceived Jesus, the Savior. Other instances where the Holy Spirit is present in the New Testament include Jesus' baptism, when the Holy Spirit descends like a dove (see Luke 3:21–22), and when John the Baptist promises his followers that Jesus will baptize with the Holy Spirit (see Matthew 3:11). Later in the Gospels, Jesus himself promises his disciples that the Father will send them an Advocate, the Holy Spirit, in his name, to be with them always (see John 14:16, 26). This promise was fulfilled on the first Pentecost, when the Holy Spirit descended on the Apostles, with Mary present among them. This event is sometimes called the birth of the Church, because it was then that, through the work of the Holy Spirit, the Apostles were able to begin their work of **evangelization** and to baptize in Jesus' name. The Holy Spirit continues to build up the Church and make it holy.

In the Gospels, as in the Church today, the role of the Holy Spirit, the Third Person of the Blessed Trinity, is interconnected with that of Jesus. Whenever God the Father sends the Son, he also sends his Spirit. While each has a unique role, their mission is the same, and together they build up the Church and make it holy.

CATECHISM Q&A

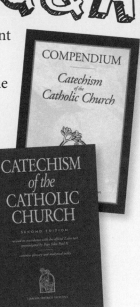

Q. What symbols are used to represent the Holy Spirit?

A. Symbols for the Holy Spirit include the *dove*, which descended on Jesus at his baptism; *fire*, which transforms what it touches; *living water*, which quenches the thirst of the baptized; and *anointing* with oil, as is done in the Sacrament of Confirmation. (See *Compendium*, Question 139; *CCC*, 964–701.)

Q. What is the work of the Holy Spirit in Mary?

A. All the waiting and preparation of the Old Testament for the coming of the Messiah was fulfilled in Mary. Mary conceived the Son of God by the power of the Holy Spirit; as the mother of the Son of God she became the mother of the whole Church. (See *Compendium*, Question 142; *CCC*, 744.)

Calendar Connection
Vatican II

WHO Pope John XXIII and 2,500 bishops from around the world

WHAT The Second Vatican Council

WHEN October 11, 1962 (opening day) until 1965

WHERE St. Peter's Basilica in Rome

WHY To reaffirm the unchanging truths of the Catholic Church and to examine ways to communicate them to people in the modern world

KNOW and BELIEVE

When the Apostles received the Holy Spirit they found the wisdom and the courage to express their beliefs. Describe a situation you might encounter with your friends or peers when you would benefit from the help of the Holy Spirit.

_____

_____

_____

_____

KNOW iT!

evangelization
the proclaiming of the Good News of Jesus and the love of God through word and witness

SAINTLY *profiles*

The Holy Spirit descended upon the Apostles and enabled them to share the Good News of Jesus with all people and to be understood by them. In the same way, the Holy Spirit has helped many saints as well as ordinary people to work for the Church and strengthen it. Saint Catherine of Siena is one of these people.

Saint Catherine of Siena 1347–1380

Catherine of Siena was born in 1347 in Siena, Italy. At age sixteen, Catherine joined the Dominican Third Order, and devoted as much of her time as possible to prayer. At age twenty she felt called by God to abandon her life of solitude and to become active in the world.

Catherine's most important response to this call was in helping resolve conflicts about the papacy. Although from the time of the early Church the Pope had resided in Rome, since 1309, popes had lived in Avignon, in France, and were believed to be completely under French control. Through her extensive correspondence with Pope Gregory XI, Catherine was able to persuade him to return to Rome from Avignon in 1377.

Although Catherine never had any formal education, she had a brilliant mind and was known for her wisdom and wrote with great insight on matters of theology.

ALL ABOUT
SAINT CATHERINE OF SIENA

* The youngest of twenty-five children of a wool dyer from Siena, Italy
* As a Dominican tertiary, or lay member of the Dominican Order, cared for cancer patients, lepers, and condemned prisoners
* Known for advising popes and for her great writings
* Her *Dialogues of Saint Catherine* among the most brilliant writings in the Church
* Suffered a stroke and died at age 33
* Relics enshrined in Siena and Venice
* Canonized in 1461

FEAST DAY: April 29 **PATRONAGE:** Rome, Europe, headache sufferers

MAKE IT HAPPEN

When the Church was threatened by the conflict over the papacy, Catherine of Siena worked to help resolve the conflict. As Catholics, we are all called to work for the good of the Church, yet our role doesn't have to be as impressive as Saint Catherine's. We can make simpler contributions, starting at our own parishes.

Describe one way you can get involved at your parish to help it in its work of evangelization.

_____

_____

_____

_____

_____

KNOW IT!

Ichthus (IK'thes)

"Ichthus" is a Greek word meaning "fish." Early Christians used the term to represent the phrase "Jesus Christ, God's Son, Savior." In Greek, the first letter of each word in that phrase spells "ichthus," or *fish*.

YOUR TURN

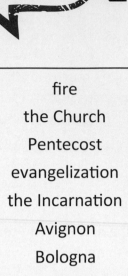

LESSON 4

A. Complete the following sentences, using words from the box. Not all words will be used.

1 The day on which the Holy Spirit came to Jesus' disciples is _____ .

2 The proclaiming of the Good News of Jesus and the love of God through word and witness is called _____ .

3 _____ is one of the symbols used to represent the Holy Spirit.

4 The Holy Spirit's greatest participation in God's work of salvation can be witnessed in the New Testament, beginning with _____ .

5 Saint Catherine of Siena convinced Pope Gregory XI to move back to Rome from _____ .

6 Together, Jesus and the Holy Spirit build up _____ and make it holy.

fire
the Church
Pentecost
evangelization
the Incarnation
Avignon
Bologna
water

B. Respond to the following.

In what ways did Saint Catherine of Siena contribute to the work of building up the Church?

_____

_____

_____

How can you use your mind and intellect to work for the good of the Church?

_____

_____

_____

One Holy Catholic and Apostolic Church

A Prayer for the Church

Side 1: Rise up in splendor! Your light has come, the glory of the LORD shines upon you.

Side 2: See, darkness covers the earth, and thick clouds cover the peoples;

Side 1: But upon you the LORD shines, and over you appears his glory.

Side 2: Nations shall walk by your light and kings by your shining radiance.

—Isaiah 60:1–4

Live It Out
As members of the Church, we are called to lead others to Christ. How do you do that in your interactions with family and friends?

BIBLE BOOST

> "Go, therefore, and make disciples of all nations, baptizing them in the name of the Father, and of the Son, and of the holy Spirit."

The Commissioning of the Disciples

Before Jesus returned to his Father in Heaven, he commissioned his disciples to continue his work on earth, teaching others all that he himself taught and baptizing them as his followers. He also gave the disciples, and therefore us, reassurance that he is always present among us.

Christ Calling His Disciples, Adam Brenner, 1839 (oil on canvas, Austria)

SACRED SCRIPTURE

A READING FROM THE HOLY GOSPEL ACCORDING TO MATTHEW

The eleven disciples went to Galilee, to the mountain to which Jesus had ordered them. When they saw him, they worshiped, but they doubted. Then Jesus approached and said to them, "All power in heaven and on earth has been given to me. Go, therefore, and make disciples of all nations, baptizing them in the name of the Father, and of the Son, and of the holy Spirit, teaching them to observe all that I have commanded you. And behold, I am with you always, until the end of the age."

—Matthew 28:16–20

START LIVING

Jesus commanded the Apostles to "make disciples of all nations," and they responded by traveling throughout the Roman Empire to preach the Gospel. As a disciple of Jesus, you are also called to make disciples, but you don't have to travel to faraway places to do so.

What are some simple ways that you can lead others to Jesus in your everyday life?

Who in your life has played an especially important part in helping you grow as a disciple of Jesus?

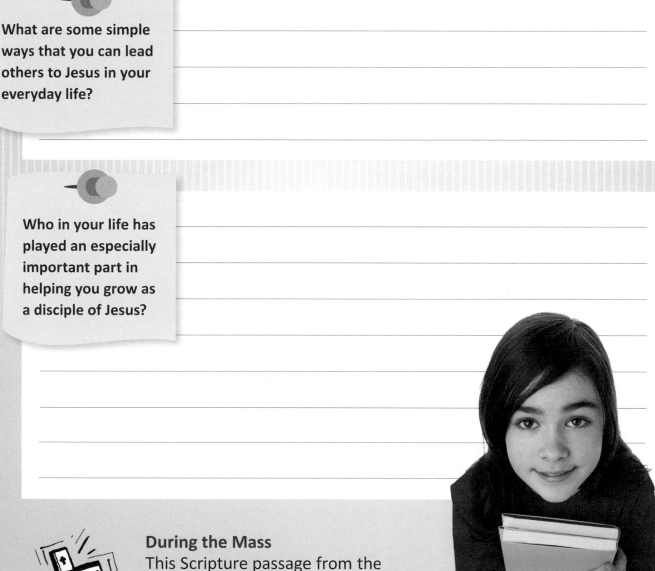

During the Mass
This Scripture passage from the Gospel of Matthew is the closing passage of that Gospel. It is read on the Feast of the Ascension during Year A. See pages 218–219.

OUR CATHOLIC TRADITION

The Church Founded by Jesus Christ

The Catholic Church today is made of people from all over the world, on all continents, speaking countless languages. It is led by the Pope, the successor of Saint Peter and the Bishop of Rome, and the bishops. The Church as it is today is the same Church founded by Jesus and led by the first disciples.

The word *church* means "convocation," or a gathering of people called together for a specific purpose. The Church is the gathering of the People of God, called by him, with the help of the Holy Spirit, and is both a sign and instrument of salvation. The Church continues Christ's mission to bring the Good News of salvation to others. Through Baptism, we become members of the People of God, the Church, called to live as one family, following the commandments that Jesus gave us.

The Catholic Church is both a visible and spiritual expression of Christ's love; therefore, she is both human and divine. She is the Bride of Christ because in his love for her Christ sacrificed his life. The Church is the Body of Christ, united but made up of many members. In the Nicene Creed, we express our belief in the essential qualities of the Church, that it is One, Holy, Catholic, and Apostolic. These qualities are called the **Marks of the Church**. We say that the Church is One because she acknowledges one Lord, confesses one faith, and forms one body. The Church is Holy because she is united with God, with Christ as her head, guided by the Holy Spirit; Catholic, or universal, because she contains all the truths of salvation and has a mission to all people; and Apostolic because she is founded on the Apostles, and continues to be led by the Apostles through their successors, the Pope and the bishops. This is called **Apostolic Succession**, and can be traced to the Scriptures, when Jesus said to his disciples, "As the Father has sent me, so I send you" (John 20:21). When all the bishops of the world in union with the Pope, called the Magisterium, speak on matters of faith and morals, their teachings are guided by the Holy Spirit and are without error. This is called **Infallibility**, and is for us a divine guarantee that their teachings represent the truths of salvation. The Magisterium communicates to us the teachings of our faith, and instructs us in how to apply them to our lives.

CATECHISM Q&A

Q. What does it mean when we say that outside the Church there is no salvation?

A. All salvation comes from Christ, through the Church. However, those who through no fault of their own do not know the Gospel of Christ or his Church but sincerely seek God can attain eternal salvation. (See *Compendium*, Question 171; *CCC*, 846, 847.)

Q. What is the mission of the Pope?

A. The Pope is the Bishop of Rome and the successor of Saint Peter. He is the perpetual, visible source and foundation of the unity of the Church. He is the vicar of Christ, the head of the College of Bishops, and pastor of the universal Church, and has universal power in the care of souls. (See *Compendium*, Question 182; *CCC*, 936, 937.)

CATHOLIC CUSTOMS
WEEK OF PRAYER FOR CHRISTIAN UNITY

Each new year, from January 18 to 25, the Church participates in the Week of Prayer for Christian Unity. During this week, Christians from many denominations come together to engage in dialogue and to pray that the divisions in Christianity may end, so that Jesus' hope "that all may be one" may become a reality.

KNOW and BELIEVE

The Church is the Body of Christ, made up of many members, each with individual gifts and talents to contribute. What are your special gifts or abilities that you can use for the good of the Church?

_____

_____

_____

_____

_____

_____

KNOW IT!

Marks of the Church
the four characteristics of Christ's Church: One, Holy, Catholic, and Apostolic, as professed in the Nicene Creed

Apostolic Succession
the unbroken passing of the mission and authority of the Apostles to their successors, the bishops

Infallibility
the gift given by the Holy Spirit to the Pope and the bishops in union with him to teach on matters of faith and morals without error

SAINTLY *profiles*

The Pope, also called the vicar of Christ, is the direct successor of the apostle Peter. As the first Pope and the apostle chosen by Christ to lead his Church, Saint Peter holds a place of great importance in the Church.

Saint Peter d. first century

Peter's discipleship began when Jesus called him and his brother Andrew, both fishermen on the Sea of Galilea, to follow him and be "fishers of men."

Saint Peter was always one of Jesus' closest disciples, and was with him during some of the most important events of his ministry, including the Transfiguration (see Matthew 17:1–8) and the Agony in the Garden of Gethsemane (see Matthew 26:36–41). Still, Peter was not always a perfect disciple. When Jesus asked him to stay awake with him while he prayed in the Garden of Gethsemane on the night before he died, Peter could not resist the urge to sleep. He showed even greater weakness when three times on the night before Jesus died, he denied being one of his followers (see Matthew 26:69–75). Yet Peter deeply regretted having betrayed Jesus, and wept in remorse.

Despite Peter's human weakness, Jesus saw in him the commitment to his mission and the strength to lead the disciples and his Church. It was Peter among all the disciples who acknowledged Jesus as the Messiah, the Son of the living God (Matthew 16:16). Christ responded to this by appointing Peter the head of his Church: "You are Peter, and upon this rock I will build my church.... I will give you the keys to the kingdom of heaven. Whatever you bind on earth shall be bound in heaven; and whatever you loose on earth shall be loosed in heaven" (Matthew 16:18–19).

ALL ABOUT
SAINT PETER

* Before becoming Jesus' disciple, was named Simon

* Jesus changed his name to Peter, from a Greek word meaning "rock"

* Recognized as the leader of the Apostles and the first Pontiff, or Pope, from the earliest days of the Church

* Martyred by being crucified upside down

FEAST DAY: June 29; also honored on February 22, the Feast of the Chair of Saint Peter

MAKE IT HAPPEN

Jesus chose Saint Peter for a role of great responsibility and importance: to lead his Church. However, Saint Peter was not always an ideal disciple of Jesus. He went so far as to deny being a follower of Jesus.

How does Saint Peter's story give you encouragement in living out your faith?

_____

_____

_____

_____

_____

Catholic Social Teaching
CALL TO FAMILY, COMMUNITY, AND PARTICIPATION

In order for our society to be healthy, we must all make positive contributions to it, bringing to it the light of the Gospels. We can do this by finding practical ways to participate more fully in our own families, in our parishes, and in our communities.

What is a way that you can more fully participate in family life? In what way can you be more active in your parish? Make a commitment to put these ideas into practice.

LET US PRAY

A Blessing Prayer
Show favor, O Lord, to your servants and mercifully increase the gifts of your grace,
that, made fervent in hope, faith and charity,
they may be ever watchful in keeping your commands.
—Opening Prayer, Sixteenth Sunday in Ordinary Time, Roman Missal

YOUR TURN

A. Circle the letter of the best answer.

1 Because the Catholic Church is both a visible and spiritual expression of Christ's love, she is both _____ .

a universal and communal

b human and divine

c papal and holy

d one and apostolic

2 The four characteristics of Christ's Church that distinguish it as One, Holy, Catholic, and Apostolic, as we profess in the Nicene Creed, are called _____ .

a Apostolic Succession

b holiness

c Infallibility

d the Marks of the Church

3 The idea that the Church is founded on the Apostles and continues to be led through their successors, the Pope and the bishops, is called _____ .

a Apostolic Succession

b Infallibility

c communion

d the vicar of Christ

4 The gift given by the Holy Spirit to the Pope and the bishops in union with him to teach on matters of faith without error is called _____ .

a Apostolic Succession

b salvation

c Infallibility

d Christian unity

5 The Church is called catholic, or universal, because _____ .

a she is present throughout the world

b she is united with God, with Christ as her head, guided by the Holy Spirit

c Mass is celebrated in every language

d she contains all the truths of salvation and has a mission to all people

6 Peter's discipleship began _____ .

a at the Resurrection

b when Jesus called him to be a "fisher of men"

c when Jesus commissioned the disciples

d when he denied Jesus three times

B. Respond to the following.

Why does Saint Peter hold a place of great importance in the Church?

_____

_____

_____

Describe two ways that you can follow Saint Peter's example in your own life.

_____

_____

The Virgin Mary

Praying with the Magnificat

My soul proclaims the
greatness of the LORD;
    my spirit rejoices in
    God my savior.
The Mighty One has done
great things for me,
    and holy is his name.

—Luke 1:46, 49

Live It Out

Mary's acceptance of God's will makes her a perfect model for how we should respond to God. Who in your life has been an example for you of how to be open to God's will?

BIBLE BOOST

> *"Do not be afraid, Mary, for you have found favor with God."*

The Announcement of the Birth of Jesus

In the Gospel of Luke, we read the account of the **Annunciation**, the angel Gabriel's announcement to the Virgin Mary that she would be the mother of the Son of God. By saying yes to her role in the birth of Jesus, Mary began her cooperation with God's work of salvation.

SACRED SCRIPTURE

A READING FROM THE HOLY GOSPEL ACCORDING TO LUKE

The angel Gabriel was sent from God to a town of Galilee called Nazareth, to a virgin betrothed to a man named Joseph, of the house of David, and the virgin's name was Mary. And coming to her, he said, "Hail, favored one! The Lord is with you." But she was greatly troubled at what was said and pondered what sort of greeting this might be. Then the angel said to her, "Do not be afraid, Mary, for you have found favor with God. Behold, you will conceive in your womb and bear a son, and you shall name him Jesus. He will be great and will be called Son of the Most High, and the Lord God will give him the throne of David his father, and he will rule over the house of Jacob forever, and of his kingdom there will be no end." But Mary said to the angel, "How can this be, since I have no relations with a man?" And the angel said to her in reply, "The holy Spirit will come upon you, and the power of the Most High will overshadow you. Therefore the child to be born will be called holy, the Son of God. And behold, Elizabeth, your relative, has also conceived a son in her old age, and this is the sixth month for her who was called barren; for nothing will be impossible for God." Mary said, "Behold, I am the handmaid of the Lord. May it be done to me according to your word." Then the angel departed from her.

—Luke 1:26–38

The Annunciation, Fra Angelico, 1438–1440 (fresco, Florence)

START LIVING

When the angel Gabriel appeared to Mary and announced to her that she would be the mother of the Son of God, Mary felt unsure of what his words meant and of how to respond. In the end, however, she accepted God's will, leaving all to his wisdom and care.

When we face challenging situations in our own lives, we may find it difficult to accept that God truly knows what is best for us. **Describe a challenging situation a young person your age might face and how trust in God can make it easier to accept.**

The result of Mary's surrender to God's will was the birth of Jesus, the Savior. **What can you learn from Mary's example that can help you in your own life?**

Stop and Think

Choose a phrase from the Scripture reading that can guide you when you are unsure about how to respond to God's will. How can this phrase guide you in your response to God?

KNOW IT!

Annunciation
the Angel Gabriel's announcement to the Virgin Mary that she was called to be the Mother of God

"Blessed are you who believed that what was spoken to you by the Lord would be fulfilled."

—Luke 1:45

Mary, Mother of God

The Virgin Mary was an important part of God's plan for our salvation. In the Old Testament, the prophet Isaiah said of her, "Therefore the Lord himself will give you this sign: the virgin will be with child, and bear a son, and shall name him Immanuel" (Isaiah 7:14). To prepare Mary for her special role as the mother of his divine Son, he made her free from **Original Sin** from the moment she was conceived. This is known as the **Immaculate Conception**. Mary was in a perfect state of grace from the first moment she came into being and remained free from sin throughout her life. Because of this, she was able to cooperate in God's plan for our salvation.

According to God's plan, Jesus Christ was born of a virgin, conceived by the power of the Holy Spirit. Mary had no children other than Jesus and remained a virgin throughout her life. Because Jesus is truly the Son of God and also one with God, the Church has given Mary the title *Theotokos*, meaning "God-bearer," to affirm that she is not only the Mother of the Son of God made man, who is God himself, but also the Mother of God.

Mary is also the spiritual mother of us all and the mother of the Church. We can find the roots of this belief in the Scriptures, when Jesus said to Mary, "Woman, behold, your son," and to the apostle John, "Behold, your mother." (John 19:26–27.)

The Assumption, Titian, 1510 (fresco, Florence)

Because of Mary's faithfulness to God, when she died she was taken up into Heaven body and soul. This event is called the **Assumption**, and the Church in America commemorates it on August 15.

CATECHISM Q&A

Q. In what sense is the Virgin Mary the Mother of the Church?

A. Mary is the Mother of the Church because she gave birth to Jesus, the Son of God, who is the Head of the Church. (See *Compendium*, Question 196; *CCC*, 973.)

Q. How does the Virgin Mary help the Church?

A. After her Assumption into Heaven, Mary continues to intercede for her children, and to be a model of faith and charity for all. Catholics see in her an image of the resurrection that awaits them and they invoke her as advocate and helper. (See *Compendium*, Question 197; *CCC*, 975.)

KNOW and BELIEVE

What inspires you about Mary, and how can she be an example for you in your own life?

_____

_____

_____

_____

_____

Calendar Connection
Doctrine of the Assumption

WHO Pope Pius XII

WHAT Doctrine of the Assumption

WHERE The Vatican, Rome

WHEN November 1, 1950

WHY Catholics had long believed that the Blessed Virgin Mary was taken body and soul into Heaven when she died. However, it was not until All Saints' Day in 1950 that the Assumption was declared to be a dogma, or official belief and teaching of the Church, by Pope Pius XII.

KNOW iT!

Original Sin
the sin of the first man and woman, passed on to all people, through which we are weakened in our ability to resist sin

Immaculate Conception
the truth that Mary was free from Original Sin and all sin from the moment she was conceived

Assumption
the teaching that when the Virgin Mary's earthly life ended she was taken up body and soul into Heaven

SAINTLY *profiles*

Through the centuries, the Virgin Mary has appeared to many holy people. Often, these people were of humble origins—peasants or children. One such person chosen by Mary to bring her and her Son's message of salvation into the world is Saint Juan Diego, in fifteenth-century Mexico.

Saint Juan Diego 1474–1548

Juan Diego, a native of Mexico, was baptized into the Christian faith at about age fifty. On December 9, 1531, while Juan Diego was walking to Mass, the Virgin Mary appeared to him on Tepeyac Hill, near what today is Mexico City. Mary appeared as a young, pregnant native woman, and spoke to Juan Diego in his own language. She revealed herself to him as Mary, the Mother of God.

Calling Juan Diego "Juanito," Mary asked him to go to the local bishop and request that he build a church on the site where she appeared. When Juan Diego did as Mary had asked, the bishop was skeptical. He told Juan Diego to provide a sign that his request truly came from Mary.

On December 12, before Juan Diego could return to Tepeyac Hill to appeal to Mary for a sign, he was traveling to see his dying uncle. Along the way, Mary met Juan Diego and told him that his uncle was cured. She then asked him to go to the hill and gather flowers to bring to the bishop as a sign. Juan Diego did as Mary instructed, and although there were normally no flowers in bloom at that time, he found roses that he could collect. He wrapped them in his *tilma*, or cloak, and brought them to the bishop. When he unfolded his *tilma*, he and the bishop were amazed to see Mary's image imprinted on the cloak. She looked just as Juan Diego had described her.

ALL ABOUT
SAINT JUAN DIEGO

* Baptized by Franciscan missionaries who had recently arrived in Mexico

* Lived his later years as a hermit near Mary's shrine on Tepeyac Hill

* Canonized by Pope John Paul II in 2002

FEAST DAY: December 9
FEAST OF OUR LADY OF GUADALUPE: December 12

The bishop acknowledged the miracle and ordered a shrine to be built where Mary had appeared, and where the cloak would be housed. News of Mary's apparition quickly spread through Mexico, and in the years that followed, millions of natives were baptized into the Catholic faith.

The Basilica of Our Lady of Guadalupe in Mexico City is the second most visited Catholic shrine in the world. *Nuestra Señora de Guadalupe* (Our Lady of Guadalupe) is the most popular devotion among Mexican people and is commonly recognized as a symbol of Mexico.

MAKE IT HAPPEN

Through Juan Diego's vision of the Virgin Mary, and his cooperation with her, the Catholic faith and devotion to the Virgin Mary grew throughout Mexico.

Describe a faith experience that you have had that you felt compelled to share with others.

_____

_____

_____

_____

_____

LET US PRAY

Memorare

Remember, O most gracious Virgin Mary, that never was it known that anyone who fled to thy protection, implored thy help, or sought thy intercession was left unaided. Inspired by this confidence I fly unto thee, O Virgin of virgins, my Mother. To thee do I come, before thee I stand, sinful and sorrowful. O Mother of the Word Incarnate, despise not my petitions, but in thy mercy hear and answer me. Amen.

KNOW IT!

Chi Rho (KEE Ro)
This is an ancient symbol for Christ that comes from the first two letters in the Greek word for Christ, X (chi) and P (rho).

YOUR TURN

A. Complete the following sentences, using words from the box.

1 According to God's plan, Jesus Christ was born of a virgin, conceived by the power of the _____ .

2 The angel Gabriel's announcement to the Virgin Mary that she would be the mother of the Son of God is called the _____ .

3 The Church has given Mary the title _____ , meaning "God-bearer."

4 On August 15, the Church in America commemorates the Feast of the _____ , Mary's being taken body and soul into Heaven.

5 The doctrine of the _____ affirms that Mary was free from Original Sin from the moment she was conceived.

6 The sin of the first man and woman, passed on to all people, through which we are weakened in our ability to resist sin is called _____ .

> Annunciation
> Immaculate Conception
> Holy Spirit
> *Theotokos*
> Original Sin
> Assumption

B. Respond to the following.

How is the Virgin Mary an important part of God's plan for salvation?

_____

_____

_____

In what ways can the Virgin Mary help you realize God's plan for you?

_____

_____

_____

Life Everlasting

A Prayer of Hope

In you, LORD, I take refuge;
  let me never be put to shame.
Be my rock and refuge,
  my secure stronghold;
  for you are my rock and fortress.
My mouth shall be filled with your praise,
  shall sing your glory every day.

—Psalm 71:1, 3, 8

Live It Out

At the end of our lives, God will judge us according to how well we have loved him, others, and ourselves. In what ways can you grow in love for God? for others? for yourself?

BIBLE BOOST

> "For I was hungry and you gave me food, I was thirsty and you gave me drink, a stranger and you welcomed me, naked and you clothed me, ill and you cared for me, in prison and you visited me."

The Judgment of the Nations

In the Gospel of Matthew, we read several parables in which Jesus tells about the Last Judgment, when those who have been faithful servants and followers of Jesus will receive their eternal reward, while those who have not will receive eternal punishment. In the following Scripture passage, Jesus talks about how, when he returns at the end of time, all people will be judged according to how they lived.

The Last Judgment, John Bellegambe the Elder, c. 1525 (oil on panel, Netherlands)

SACRED SCRIPTURE

A READING FROM THE HOLY GOSPEL ACCORDING TO MATTHEW

"When the Son of Man comes in his glory, and all the angels with him, he will sit upon his glorious throne, and all the nations will be assembled before him. And he will separate them one from another, as a shepherd separates the sheep from the goats. He will place the sheep on his right and the goats on his left. Then the king will say to those on his right, 'Come, you who are blessed by my Father. Inherit the kingdom prepared for you from the foundation of the world. For I was hungry and you gave me food, I was thirsty and you gave me drink, a stranger and you welcomed me, naked and you clothed me, ill and you cared for me, in prison and you visited me.' Then the righteous will answer him and say, 'Lord, when did we see you hungry and feed you, or thirsty and give you drink? When did we see you a stranger and welcome you, or naked and clothe you? When did we see you ill or in prison, and visit you?' And the king will say to them in reply, 'Amen, I say to you, whatever you did for one of the least brothers of mine, you did for me.' Then he will say to those on his left, 'Depart from me, you accursed, into the eternal fire prepared for the devil and his angels. For I was hungry and you gave me no food, I was thirsty and you gave me no drink, a stranger and you gave me no welcome, naked and you gave me no clothing, ill and in prison, and you did not care for me.' Then they will answer and say, 'Lord, when did we see you hungry or thirsty or a stranger or naked or ill or in prison, and not minister to your needs?' He will answer them, 'Amen, I say to you, what you did not do for one of these least ones, you did not do for me.' And these will go off to eternal punishment, but the righteous to eternal life."

—Matthew 25:31–46

START LIVING

Jesus tells us that at the end of our lives, we will be judged according to our deeds during our lifetime. He especially stresses the importance of caring for others and seeing him in all people.

How can you carry out Jesus' instruction to care for those who are hungry or thirsty?

How can you follow Jesus' instruction to care for the ill or those in prison?

During the Mass
This Scripture passage from Matthew's Gospel about the Last Judgment is read on the Feast of Christ the King, the last Sunday in the Liturgical Year, during Year A. See pages 218–219.

OUR CATHOLIC TRADITION

We Believe in Everlasting Life

Most people do not like to think about death, seeing in it an end rather than a beginning. Of course, death is the end of our physical life on earth; however, our faith tells us that it is also the start of a new life.

When we die, our souls are separated from our bodies, but at our resurrection on the last day God will give incorruptible life to our bodies and reunite them with our soul. At the time of our death, we undergo a personal, or particular, judgment in which we receive either the eternal reward of Heaven or the eternal punishment of Hell. **Heaven** and Hell are a state either of eternal happiness with God or eternal separation from him. In Heaven, we will be in a perfect relationship with the Blessed Trinity, and will share in the joy of this relationship with the Virgin Mary, and all the angels and saints. Angels are spiritual creatures who exist to serve and glorify God and to cooperate in his plan for our salvation.

The Last Judgment, Michelangelo Buonarroti, c. 1539 (fresco, Sistine Chapel)

Through his death and Resurrection, Jesus Christ made it possible for us to share in the reward of Heaven. Of course, most people do not die in a state of perfect holiness. Therefore, before entering Heaven, souls often must undergo a period of purification to achieve the holiness necessary for eternal joy with God in Heaven. This purification is called **Purgatory**.

Those who fail to love God and freely choose to commit serious sin against him or against their neighbor or themselves are subject to eternal death, or **Hell**. These souls must endure unending separation from God. Whereas each person faces a particular judgment immediately after death, at the end of time, when Christ returns in glory, a **Last Judgment** will occur in which all will be raised from the dead and will appear before Christ, to receive their eternal reward or eternal punishment. At that time, the Kingdom of God will come in its fullness, and the just will reign with Christ forever, glorified in body and soul. Faith is essential for salvation; we cannot achieve eternal happiness with God if we do not have faith in his promises and freely choose to love him. The Church, as the **Communion of Saints**, seeks the salvation of all people, and entrusts the dead to God's mercy and prays for their eternal reward in Heaven. Although the Church prays for the souls in Purgatory at every Mass, we remember them in a special way on the second day of November, the Feast of All Souls' Day.

CATECHISM Q&A

Q. How can we reconcile the existence of Hell with the infinite goodness of God?

A. God calls all people to union with him; however, he created us to be free and responsible for our own decisions. Therefore, if at the moment of death a person persists in grave sin and refuses God's mercy, that person has freely chosen eternal separation from God. (See *Compendium*, Question 213; *CCC*, 1033–1034, 1037.)

Q. When will the Last, or Final, Judgment occur?

A. This judgment will come at the end of the world. Only God knows the hour and the day. (See *Compendium*, Question 215; *CCC*, 1038.)

CATHOLIC CUSTOMS THE BOOK OF REMEMBRANCE

In the month of November, when the Feast of All Souls' Day is celebrated, many parishes provide a Book of Remembrance where parishioners can inscribe the names of deceased relatives and friends. This practice is about more than just remembering; it is an occasion to help souls in Purgatory reach the gift of Heaven through our prayers, alms, and works of penance.

KNOW and BELIEVE

The Church's teachings and Scriptures tell us that at the end of time we will be judged according to how we have lived. How does this affect how you live your life?

_____

_____

_____

_____

_____

KNOW IT!

Heaven
everlasting happiness with God and with the Virgin Mary and all the angels and saints

Purgatory
a final purification from sin after death, which one may need before entry into Heaven

Hell
everlasting separation from God, reserved for those who freely and consciously reject him

Communion of Saints
the spiritual union of all believers, who form one body in Christ

SAINTLY *profiles*

God calls all of us to a life of everlasting happiness with him and with all the angels and saints. Although the path to this eternal happiness can pose challenges for us to overcome each day, it does not require heroism or extreme acts of self-sacrifice. As we can learn from the example of Saint Thérèse of Lisieux, we can achieve holiness in simple ways, as long as we have great love for God.

Saint Thérèse of Lisieux
1873–1897

Thérèse of Lisieux, also known as the "Little Flower," was born in Alençon, France. She was the ninth child born into the Martin family. From a young age Thérèse had a strong desire do God's will and felt called to serve him by joining the Carmelites as a nun. At age 15, although still very young for entering religious life, Thérèse received permission from her bishop to enter the convent, and joined two of her older sisters there.

At first, Thérèse found convent life difficult, but by accepting the daily challenges, she was strengthened to serve God humbly and obediently. Thérèse's life of prayer as a young Carmelite became known after her death through her autobiography, *The Story of a Soul.* Thérèse's superiors, seeing in her a unique holiness, encouraged her to write this book. In it, she describes her "little way" to sainthood, emphasizing the importance of great love rather than great deeds. This notion is based on the idea that God welcomes those who are spiritually childlike and show complete confidence in his love. Thérèse herself was an example of this relationship with God. She said, "I tell God what I want quite simply, without any splendid turns of phrase, and somehow he always manages to understand me."

ALL ABOUT
SAINT THÉRÈSE

- ✻ Died at age twenty-four, after years of suffering with tuberculosis

- ✻ Her "little way" to sainthood has inspired millions to imitate her in striving to attain holiness in living an ordinary life

- ✻ Canonized in 1925

- ✻ Declared a Doctor of the Church in 1997

- ✻ In 2008, both of her parents were beatified

FEAST DAY: October 1
PATRONAGE: the missions

MAKE IT HAPPEN

Saint Thérèse teaches us that we can show love for God in ordinary ways.

Describe three everyday things that you do, then tell how you can do each in a way that shows greater love for God.

_____

_____

_____

_____

_____

Catholic Social Teaching
OPTION FOR THE POOR AND VULNERABLE

God loves all people, and he calls us to love one another as he loves us. In a world where many people live in great poverty while others enjoy great wealth, we must pay special attention to the needs of the poor and reach out to them in Christian charity.

Choose a way that you can reach out to someone in need, and put your plan into action this week.

LET US PRAY

Prayer to Our Guardian Angel
Angel of God, my guardian dear,
to whom God's love commits me here,
ever this day be at my side,
to light and guard, to rule and guide.
Amen.

YOUR TURN

LESSON 7

A. Match Column A with Column B by writing the correct letter in the space provided.

A
a. All Souls' Day
b. Hell
c. Communion of Saints
d. Heaven
e. Purgatory
f. Last Judgment

B

1. _____ the spiritual union of all believers, who form one body in Christ

2. _____ the judgment of all people by Jesus Christ at his Second Coming

3. _____ everlasting happiness with God and with all people who love him

4. _____ a solemn day of prayer for the souls in Purgatory

5. _____ a final purification from sin after death, which one may need before entry into Heaven

6. _____ everlasting separation from God, reserved for those who freely and consciously reject him

B. Respond to the following.

What does Saint Thérèse teach about what it takes to achieve sainthood?

_____

_____

_____

What does Saint Thérèse's approach to holiness teach you about how you can show greater love for God?

_____

_____

_____

Being Catholic

PERSONAL PRAYER AND SILENCE—COMMUNICATING WITH GOD

HOW DO WE COMMUNICATE?

What are some of the ways we communicate with friends or relatives who live in a different town, state, or country? In addition to traditional phone calls and letter writing, we can stay in touch via email, text messaging, and social networking Web sites. But imagine trying to maintain a long-distance relationship without any of this technology. You might find yourself becoming disconnected from the person, and eventually start to drift apart.

> "But when you pray, go to your inner room, close the door, and pray to your Father in secret…. Your Father knows what you need before you ask him."
> —Matthew 6:6, 8

Communication is an important part of maintaining a strong relationship. It is also an essential part of a good relationship with God. There are many ways we can maintain open lines of communication with God. God speaks to us when we read the Bible, through the teachings of the Church, through the Mass and homily, as well as through people in our lives who provide moral and spiritual guidance. We must be open to God's message, through whatever means he chooses to speak to us. Our communication with God also needs to be a two-way exchange. One way for us to stay in touch with God is through personal prayer and silence.

Where and when do you pray?

PERSONAL PRAYER AND SILENCE

Praying is one very important way we can talk and listen to God. Through prayer, we can ask God to guide us, thank him, praise him, and entrust all of our struggles, desires, hopes, fears, joys, and sorrows to his care. We can also pray through silence, in which we contemplatively listen for God's voice in our hearts. Just as our relationships with our family and close friends require ongoing communication to remain meaningful and strong, so does our relationship with God.

Name some distractions that can prevent you from praying. How can you overcome such distractions?

PRAYER IN OUR DAILY LIFE

One way to build a strong relationship with God is to develop a habit of praying daily. There are many ways we can pray to God and listen to him speak to us, including:

- **Traditional Prayer:** Formal prayers such as the Our Father or the Hail Mary.
- **Personal Prayer:** Speaking to God from your heart as you would a parent or close friend.
- **In Church:** Going to church on your own and praying in private.
- **Silence:** Praying in silence allows God to enter into our hearts.

Through prayer and silence, we can be open to the will of God in our lives. God the Holy Spirit, the Third Person of the Blessed Trinity, gives us the grace to live out God's will for us. When we are open to the grace of the Holy Spirit, the Fruits of the Holy Spirit will be visible in how we conduct our lives.

Fruits of the Holy Spirit

love	patience	faithfulness
joy	kindness	gentleness
peace	goodness	self-control

How can silence help you be open to God's presence? Describe some favorite places where you can spend time in silent prayer.

Worshiping

UNIT 2
Celebrating the Christian Mystery

By the grace of God, Christians ... become temples of the Holy Spirit, living stones out of which the Church is built. (CCC, 1197)

The Seven Sacraments

Baptism

Confirmation

Eucharist

Penance and Reconciliation

Holy Orders

Matrimony

Anointing of the Sick

The Mass

The Sanctus

Holy, Holy, Holy Lord God of hosts.
Heaven and earth are full of your glory.
Hosanna in the highest.
Blessed is he who comes
 in the name of the Lord.
Hosanna in the highest.

—*Roman Missal*

Live It Out
When you attend Sunday Mass, are you a participant or just a bystander? How can learning more about the Mass help you participate in it more fully?

BIBLE BOOST

> *While they were eating, he took bread, said the blessing, broke it, and gave it to them, and said, "Take it; this is my body."*

The Lord's Supper

On the night before Jesus died, he gathered with his disciples to commemorate the Passover, when God spared the Israelites from the final plague—death to all firstborns—sent to the Egyptians to convince Pharaoh to let the Israelites go. It was on this night that Jesus instituted the **Sacrament of Eucharist**, through which we are saved from eternal death and can gain eternal life.

The Last Supper, Leonardo da Vinci, 1498 (mural, Milan)

SACRED SCRIPTURE

A READING FROM THE HOLY GOSPEL ACCORDING TO MARK

On the first day of the Feast of Unleavened Bread, when they sacrificed the Passover lamb, his disciples said to him, "Where do you want us to go and prepare for you to eat the Passover?" He sent two of his disciples and said to them, "Go into the city and a man will meet you, carrying a jar of water. Follow him. Wherever he enters, say to the master of the house, 'The Teacher says, "Where is my guest room where I may eat the Passover with my disciples?"' Then he will show you a large upper room furnished and ready. Make the preparations for us there." The disciples then went off, entered the city, and found it just as he had told them; and they prepared the Passover.

While they were eating, he took bread, said the blessing, broke it, and gave it to them, and said, "Take it; this is my body." Then he took a cup, gave thanks, and gave it to them, and they all drank from it. He said to them, "This is my blood of the covenant, which will be shed for many. Amen, I say to you, I shall not drink again the fruit of the vine until the day when I drink it new in the kingdom of God." Then, after singing a hymn, they went out to the Mount of Olives.

—Mark 14:12–16, 22–26

START LIVING

The Last Supper was celebrated on the feast of Passover, which commemorates God's saving act in the Old Testament, when he spared the Israelites from the plague of death.

What parallel can you identify between the Passover and the Last Supper?

Jesus said to those gathered with him at the Last Supper and all of us today, "Take it; this is my body" (Mark 14:22). **How can you respond to Jesus' invitation?**

Stop and Think

Review the Scripture passage about the Last Supper and choose from it a phrase that helps you to reflect on the meaning of the Mass. How can these words help you prepare yourself to participate in the celebration of Sunday Mass?

OUR CATHOLIC TRADITION

> "I am the bread of life; whoever comes to me will never hunger, and whoever believes in me will never thirst."
> —John 6:35

Jesus Christ in the Eucharist

At the Last Supper, Jesus instituted the Eucharist, giving us his Body and Blood so that we may have eternal life. Early Christians celebrated the Eucharist in each others' homes, doing so in secret in times of persecution. Today, Catholics around the world gather in their local churches to celebrate the Eucharist, in diverse rites and traditions that express the same beliefs.

Although the Church celebrates **Mass** daily, Sunday, the Lord's Day, is the principal day for celebrating the Eucharist, because it is the day of the Resurrection. The Mass is the central **liturgy** of

the Church, and is the basis for most other liturgical celebrations. Through the Mass, we are united with Christ's sacrifice on the cross, offered to the Father for our salvation.

The Eucharistic celebration consists of two integral parts: the Liturgy of the Word and the Liturgy of the Eucharist. The Liturgy of the Word consists of proclaiming and listening to the Word of God through Scriptures. The Liturgy of the Eucharist includes the presentation of the bread and wine, the prayer of consecration, and Holy Communion, during which the assembly receives the Eucharist. In the Liturgy of the Eucharist, the bread and wine are consecrated by the priest and become the Body and Blood of Christ. This action is called **transubstantiation**. The Eucharist is not merely a symbol of Christ's presence; rather, Christ himself is truly present in his body and blood, soul and divinity under the appearances of bread and wine. Together, all the elements of the Liturgy of the Word and the Liturgy of the Eucharist constitute a single act of worship.

Jesus instituted the Eucharist to perpetuate his sacrifice on the cross throughout the ages, until he returns in glory. By his sacrifice he grants the grace of salvation to the Church. The Eucharist is also offered in reparation for the sins of the living and the dead, and to obtain spiritual or earthly benefits from God. Jesus entrusted the Eucharist to the Church as a memorial of his Paschal Mystery, his work of salvation through his suffering, death, Resurrection, and Ascension. We say that the Eucharist is a memorial because it makes present and real Christ's sacrifice on the Cross. The whole of the Church's liturgy, all of its worship, finds its center and most intense expression in the celebration of the Eucharist.

CATECHISM Q&A

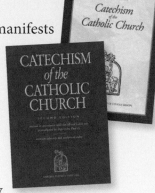

Q. What is the role of the Holy Spirit in the Liturgy of the Church?

A. The Holy Spirit prepares the assembly to encounter Christ, manifests Christ to the assembly, makes the saving work of Christ present and active, and makes the Eucharist bear fruit in the Church. (See *Compendium*, Question 223; *CCC*, 1112.)

Q. Who is at work in the liturgy of the Church?

A. The liturgy is the work of Christ, the head of the Church, and the faithful, as his body. (See *Compendium*, Question 233; *CCC*, 1187.)

Q. Who is the minister for the celebration of the Eucharist?

A. Only a validly ordained priest, acting in the name of Christ, can celebrate the Eucharist. However, it is Christ himself, acting through the ministry of the priest, who offers the Eucharistic sacrifice. (See *Compendium*, Question 278; *CCC*, 1410, 1411.)

Calendar Connection
Lateran Council IV

WHO Pope Innocent III, all the bishops of the Church, and kings and civil authorities throughout Europe

WHAT The Fourth Lateran Council, sometimes called the Great Council

WHERE Rome, Italy

WHEN 1215

WHY Among the canons, or Church laws, established by Lateran IV was the teaching on transubstantiation, affirming that the consecrated bread and wine truly become Christ's Body and Blood.

KNOW IT!

Mass
the Church's prayer of praise and thanksgiving to God the Father and its central liturgy; the celebration of the Eucharist

liturgy
the official public worship of the Church, whose center and most intense expression is the Eucharist

transubstantiation
the change of the whole substance of bread into the Body of Christ and the whole substance of wine into the Blood of Christ

KNOW and BELIEVE

When you participate in the Mass and receive Holy Communion, you are more fully joined with the Church. What are some ways that you can demonstrate that you are an active member of the Body of Christ, the Church?

_____

_____

_____

_____

SAINTLY *profiles*

In the Church's history, many people have achieved sainthood, some for their great acts of charity and service to the poor, some for their extreme holiness, and some for their work of evangelization. One thing all the saints have in common, however, is their great devotion to the Mass and the gift of the Eucharist. Padre Pio's story illustrates this devotion.

Saint Padre Pio 1887–1968

Padre Pio was born Francesco Forgione, named in honor of Saint Francis of Assisi, in the Italian village of Pietrelcina. Even as a young child, Francesco felt called to become a priest. He joined the Capuchin Friars at age fifteen, taking the name Pio in honor of Pope Saint Pius V. Eight years later he was ordained to the priesthood.

The celebration of the Mass was the center of Padre Pio's spiritual life, and through it and in all facets of his life, he lived the Passion of Christ. On September 20, 1918, as Padre Pio was kneeling in front of a large crucifix after Mass, he had a vision of Jesus. When the vision ended, he had the visible marks of the Crucifixion, called the stigmata, in his hands, feet, and side. Church authorities and medical doctors questioned and examined Padre Pio, but no natural causes for the stigmata could be found. He bore the stigmata for the rest of his life.

Padre Pio's parishioners were deeply impressed by his piety and many came to seek his spiritual guidance. For many, even a few moments in his presence proved to be a transforming experience. As the years passed, pilgrims from around the world began to come to him. He was soon hearing confessions and giving spiritual advice for more than ten hours each day.

ALL ABOUT
SAINT PADRE PIO

※ Briefly served as a chaplain in the Italian Medical Corps during World War I

※ During his lifetime and since his death, many people have reported cures they believe were received through Padre Pio's intercession

※ Canonized in 2002 with more than 300,000 people in attendance in St. Peter's Square

FEAST DAY: September 23

MAKE IT HAPPEN

Mass and the Eucharist were the center of Padre Pio's spiritual life. Describe two steps you can take to grow in your appreciation for the gift of Jesus in the Eucharist.

_____

_____

_____

_____

_____

_____

_____

KNOW IT!

Wheat and Grapes
Wheat and grapes are a symbol for the Eucharist, because it is from wheat and grapes that the bread and wine that are consecrated to become the Body and Blood of Christ are made.

LET US PRAY

A Prayer for Eternal Life
Father, by the blood of your Son you have set us free and saved us from death. Continue your work of love within us, that by constantly celebrating the mystery of our salvation we may reach the eternal life it promises. Amen.

—From the Litany of the Most Precious Blood

YOUR TURN

A. Circle the letter of the correct answer.

1 On the night before he died, Jesus instituted _____ .

a the Church

b the Sacrament of Eucharist

c the Liturgy

d Passover

2 Sunday is known as "the Lord's Day" because it is the day of the _____ .

a Transubstantiation

b Ascension

c Paschal Mystery

d Resurrection

3 _____ is the official public worship of the Church, whose center and most intense expression is the Eucharist.

a Liturgy

b Lectionary

c Eucharist

d Paschal Mystery

4 _____ is the change of the whole substance of bread into the Body of Christ and the whole substance of wine into the Blood of Christ.

a Transformation

b Transubstantiation

c Sanctus

d Holiness

5 At Mass, _____ prepares us to encounter Christ and makes Christ's saving work present and active.

a the priest

b the Holy Spirit

c transubstantiation

d the assembly

6 What are the two integral parts of the Eucharistic celebration?

a the Liturgy of the Word and the Scripture readings

b the Liturgy of the Eucharist and the presentation of the bread and wine

c the Liturgy of the Word and the Liturgy of the Eucharist

d the Scripture readings and Holy Communion

B. Respond to the following.

Describe some ways that Padre Pio demonstrated deep love for God.

_____

_____

_____

Name two ways that Padre Pio's example can help bring you closer to God.

_____

_____

Sacraments of Christian Initiation

A Prayer for Holiness

Side 1: Lord, I pray that you may be a light for me in darkness. Touch my soul and kindle a fire within it, that it may burn brightly and give light to my life, that I may truly become your temple.

Side 2: May the light within me shine on my friends that it may drive away the darkness of sin in them, too.

All: Let us be a light to the world, making visible the light of the Gospel to all those we meet. Amen.

—From a prayer by Saint Columbanus

Live It Out

As members of the Body of Christ, the Church, we are called to live Christ's message of faith, hope, and love. How are you a model of faith for others? of hope? of love?

BIBLE BOOST

And a voice came from the heavens, saying, "This is my beloved Son, with whom I am well pleased."

The Baptism of Jesus

At Jesus' baptism at the Jordan River, the Holy Spirit came upon him. It was at this event that Jesus was anointed with the Holy Spirit as Priest, sacrificing himself for the good of all people; Prophet, delivering God's message of love and forgiveness; and King, aiding those who suffer physically and spiritually. Jesus is also called Christ, meaning "Anointed One" or "Messiah," because he was anointed by the Holy Spirit. Jesus' baptism marks the beginning of his public life.

SACRED SCRIPTURE

A READING FROM THE HOLY GOSPEL ACCORDING TO MATTHEW

Jesus came from Galilee to John at the Jordan to be baptized by him. John tried to prevent him, saying, "I need to be baptized by you, and yet you are coming to me?" Jesus said to him in reply, "Allow it now, for thus it is fitting for us to fulfill all righteousness." Then he allowed him. After Jesus was baptized, he came up from the water and behold, the heavens were opened for him, and he saw the Spirit of God descending like a dove [and] coming upon him. And a voice came from the heavens, saying, "This is my beloved Son, with whom I am well pleased."

—Matthew 3:13–17

START LIVING

Although Jesus was the Son of God, free from sin and not in need of baptism, he chose to be baptized by John the Baptist. The Scriptures show us that with his baptism, Jesus began his public ministry. In a similar way, as baptized Christians we are called to serve others and the Church.

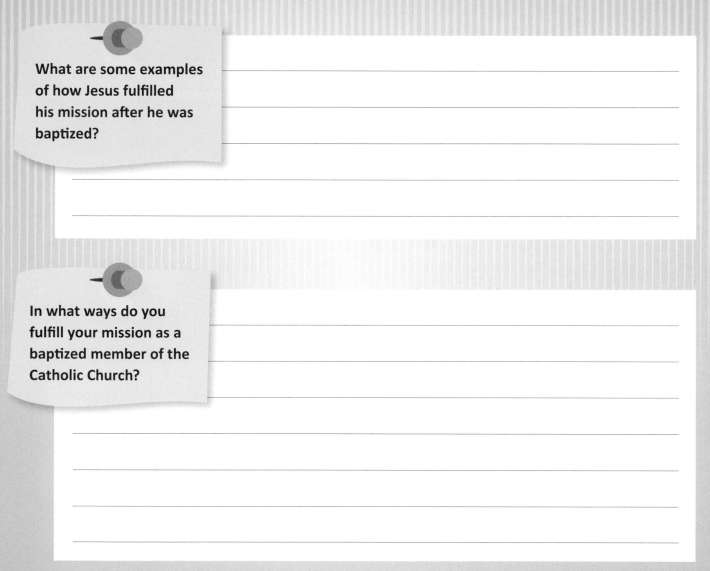

What are some examples of how Jesus fulfilled his mission after he was baptized?

In what ways do you fulfill your mission as a baptized member of the Catholic Church?

During the Mass
The Scripture reading from Matthew's Gospel about the Baptism of Jesus is read at Sunday Mass on the Feast of the Baptism of the Lord, during Year A. See pages 218–219.

OUR CATHOLIC TRADITION

New Life in Christ

In the New Testament, we read of Jesus' baptism as well as of the baptism of many new disciples (see Acts 2:37–41, for example). We read of Jesus instituting the Eucharist (see Matthew 26:26–30), and of the Holy Spirit descending upon the Apostles (see Acts 2:1–13). These **sacraments** of Baptism, Eucharist, and anointing by the Holy Spirit, or Confirmation, are the foundation of the Christian life, and are called the **Sacraments of Christian Initiation**.

In Baptism, we are born to new life in Christ and can have salvation. Through Baptism we are forgiven of **Original Sin** and all sin, and become members of the Body of Christ, the Church. Baptism is the first and chief sacrament, through which we are united to Christ and receive the Holy Spirit. Because this Sacrament imprints on our souls a permanent spiritual sign, we can only receive it once. Through Baptism, we share in Christ's priesthood and are called to exhibit the grace of the Sacrament and to witness to Christ in all aspects of our lives.

The essential rite of Baptism consists of immersing the candidate in water or pouring water on his or her head, while saying, "I baptize you in the name of the Father, and of the Son, and of the Holy Spirit." Ordinarily, the bishop, priest, or deacon is the minister of Baptism. However, in the case of an emergency, any person can baptize, provided he or she pours water over the candidate's head and prays the invocation to the Blessed Trinity. Through God's mercy, those who through no fault of their own die without being baptized can be saved.

The Sacrament of Confirmation anoints us with the Holy Spirit and perfects the grace of Baptism. Like Baptism, Confirmation imprints a permanent spiritual mark and can only be received once. The bishop is the ordinary minister of Confirmation. The essential rite of the Sacrament is the anointing on the forehead with sacred **Chrism** together with the laying on of the minister's hand and the praying of the words "Be sealed with the Gift of the Holy Spirit."

Confirmation has two main effects: It enriches us with an outpouring of the Holy Spirit and strengthens us to bear public witness to Christ in the world and more deeply unites us with Christ and the Church.

The Sacraments of Christian Initiation also include the Eucharist, which the Church has called the heart and the summit of Christian life. The Eucharist is the Sacrament of the **Real Presence** of Christ. When we receive the Eucharist, or Holy Communion, we are united with Christ, are forgiven of **venial sins**, or minor sins, and are strengthened to avoid mortal sin, or grave sin. We must not receive Holy Communion if we have committed a mortal sin that has not been forgiven in confession.

CATECHISM Q&A

Q. What is Christ's role in the Sacraments?

A. The Sacraments were all instituted by Jesus Christ. His words and actions during his hidden life and public ministry were part of his work of salvation, and announced the gift of the Sacraments he would give the Church. The mysteries of his life are the foundation for the gifts he dispenses in the Sacraments, through the action of the Holy Spirit. (See *CCC*, 1414–1416.)

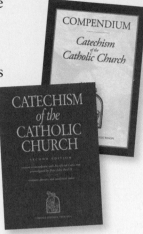

Q. Who can receive the Sacrament of Confirmation?

A. Only those who have been baptized may be confirmed. To receive Confirmation, the candidate must be in a state of grace. (See *Compendium*, Question 269; *CCC*, 1319.)

CATHOLIC CUSTOMS
RITE OF CHRISTIAN INITIATION OF ADULTS

Through the Rite of Christian Initiation of Adults (RCIA), adults who have never been baptized, called "catechumens," and those who were previously baptized in another Christian church, called "candidates for full communion," are received into the Church. The RCIA process includes catechesis, or learning about the Faith, and reception of the Sacraments of Christian Initiation.

KNOW and BELIEVE

Which of the Sacraments of Christian Initiation have you received? How do they strengthen you to live as a disciple of Christ?

_____

_____

_____

_____

_____

_____

KNOW IT!

sacrament
an efficacious sign of grace, instituted by Christ and entrusted to the Church, by which divine life is dispensed to us

Sacraments of Christian Initiation
Baptism, Confirmation, and Eucharist, the sacraments through which we enter into full membership in the Church

Original Sin
the sin of the first man and woman, passed on to all people, through which we are weakened in our ability to resist sin

SAINTLY *profiles*

In the Scriptures, we read of the Baptism of Jesus and of many other baptisms. Through the Sacrament of Baptism, we are all made members of the Church, and are called to lead others to its message of salvation. Saint Francis Xavier made this call his life's mission, traveling to faraway lands to evangelize and welcome countless people into the Church.

Saint Francis Xavier 1506–1552

Francis Xavier was born in his family's castle near Pamplona in Spain. As a young man he studied philosophy at the University of Paris, and later became a professor at the university. It was there that he met Ignatius Loyola, who convinced him to join him in founding the Society of Jesus, a religious order also known as the Jesuits.

Francis and Ignatius were ordained to the priesthood in Venice, Italy, in 1537. In 1540, when the Society of Jesus was formally recognized by the Pope, Father Francis was invited by the king of Portugal to accompany his delegation on a trip to Goa, on the west coast of India. This became the first of Francis Xavier's many missionary journeys.

After establishing a mission in Goa, Father Francis traveled to the southern tip of India, where he spent three years. He then traveled to Japan and to many parts of the Far East. Throughout his travels, Francis brought the Christian faith to countless people, and baptized thousands.

As a missionary, Francis tended to the spiritual and the physical needs of those to whom he ministered. He cared for the ill, served the poor, and taught children the Christian faith.

Francis' plans for evangelizing the Far East included a trip to China. He set off on this journey in 1552; however, he died of a fever on Shangchwan Island, off the coast of China, having never reached the mainland.

ALL ABOUT
SAINT FRANCIS XAVIER

* Considered the greatest missionary since Saint Paul
* Called the "Apostle of Japan" and the "Apostle of India"
* Canonized in 1622

PATRONAGE: All foreign missions
FEAST DAY: December 3

MAKE IT HAPPEN

Saint Francis Xavier tended to the physical and spiritual needs of people of all ages and races.

What are some ways that you can share Christ's love by caring for and helping others?

_____

_____

_____

_____

_____

_____

_____

Catholic Social Teaching
RIGHTS AND RESPONSIBILITIES

The Catholic Church teaches that every person has a right to life and the rights needed to live in dignity. As Catholics, we believe that the fundamental rights of all people are freedom, justice, and the basic necessities

of everyday life, and that as individuals and as a society we must work to protect these rights for all people.

In what way can you show respect for and defend the freedom of others?

YOUR TURN

A. Complete the following sentences, using words from the box. Not all words will be used.

1 The _____ are efficacious signs of grace, instituted by Christ and entrusted to the Church, by which divine life is dispensed to us.

2 Baptism, Confirmation, and Eucharist are _____ , through which we enter into full membership in the Church.

3 The sin of the first man and woman, passed on to all people, through which we are weakened in our ability to resist sin, is called _____ .

4 The Eucharist is the Sacrament of the _____ of Christ.

5 The Sacrament of Confirmation anoints us with the Holy Spirit and perfects the grace of _____ .

6 The ordinary minister of Confirmation is the _____ .

> Baptism
> Sacraments
> mortal sin
> Real Presence
> Original Sin
> bishop
> deacon
> Sacraments of Christian Initiation

B. Respond to the following.

What are the effects of receiving the Sacrament of the Eucharist?

_____

_____

_____

Write a short prayer that you can pray when you receive Holy Communion.

_____

_____

_____

_____

Sacraments of Healing

A Prayer for Mercy

Leader: Have mercy on me, God,
in your goodness;
in your abundant compassion
blot out my offense.

All: A clean heart create for me, God;
renew in me a steadfast spirit.

Leader: Wash away all my guilt;
from my sin cleanse me.

All: A clean heart create for me, God;
renew in me a steadfast spirit.

—Psalm 51:3, 4, 12

Live It Out

God's mercy can sustain us in our physical and spiritual needs. How does knowing that God is merciful help you reach out to him to ask for forgiveness and for help in time of need?

BIBLE BOOST

> ## "Let the one among you who is without sin be the first to throw a stone at her."

The Woman Caught in Adultery

In Old Testament times, many believed that those who sinned against the Commandments should be treated with vengeance. Jesus taught that rather than condemn the sinner, we must recognize that we are all sinners, and that God, rather than judging vengefully, wants to offer us healing and forgiveness.

Christ and the Woman Taken in Adultery, Lucas Cranach the Elder, c. 1532 (oil on canvas, Germany)

SACRED SCRIPTURE

A READING FROM THE HOLY GOSPEL ACCORDING TO JOHN

Jesus went to the Mount of Olives. But early in the morning he arrived again in the temple area, and all the people started coming to him, and he sat down and taught them. Then the scribes and the Pharisees brought a woman who had been caught in adultery and made her stand in the middle. They said to him "Teacher, this woman was caught in the very act of committing adultery. Now in the law, Moses commanded us to stone such women. So what do you say?" They said this to test him, so that they could have some charge to bring against him. Jesus bent down and began to write on the ground with his finger. But when they continued asking him, he straightened up and said to them, "Let the one among you who is without sin be the first to throw a stone at her." Again he bent down and wrote on the ground. And in response, they went away one by one, beginning with the elders. So he was left alone with the woman before him. Then Jesus straightened up and said to her, "Woman, where are they? Has no one condemned you?" She replied, "No one, sir." Then Jesus said, "Neither do I condemn you. Go, [and] from now on do not sin any more."

—John 8:1–11

START LIVING

Through his compassion to the woman caught in adultery, Jesus teaches us about his willingness to forgive sins. He also shows us how we must treat those who have sinned, whether against us or against God's laws.

What does the Scripture story of the woman caught in adultery teach you about turning to God when you have sinned?

What does it teach you about how to treat others who sin against you or against God?

Stop and Think

Rather than show scorn for the sinful woman, Jesus said to her, "Neither do I condemn you. Go, [and] from now on do not sin any more" (John 8:1–11). How can Jesus' words help you turn to God when you have sinned?

OUR CATHOLIC TRADITION

God Offers Us Forgiveness and Healing

As the story of the woman who committed adultery shows us, God is forgiving and does not seek to punish us, but to save us. After Baptism, in which we are cleansed of Original Sin and any sins we may have committed, God offers us forgiveness through the **Sacrament of Penance and Reconciliation**, one of the two **Sacraments of Healing**.

We must always obey the judgment of our **conscience** about what is morally right. We have an obligation to learn God's will and the teachings of the Church to properly form our conscience. If our conscience is well formed, we are able to make judgments according to the will of God; otherwise, we

risk committing a sin.

Sin is an utterance, a deed, or a desire that is contrary to God's law. It wounds human nature and human solidarity. There are two kinds of sin: mortal sin and venial sin. **Mortal sin** is a conscious and free choice to commit a serious violation of God's law. It is called "mortal," meaning "deadly," because it separates us from God's grace. If we die without seeking forgiveness for a mortal sin, we face separation from God for all eternity. A **venial sin** is a less serious offense against God. It does not separate us from God's grace, but weakens our relationship with him and with the Church community, and weakens our ability to resist mortal sin.

Before receiving the Sacrament of Penance, we must experience true repentence for the sins we have committed, and be firmly committed to avoiding them in the future. To receive forgiveness, or absolution, we must confess our sins to a priest after carefully examining our conscience. We are required to confess mortal sins. Although we do not have to confess venial sins, doing so strengthens us to avoid them in the future and is strongly recommended by the Church. Once we have confessed our sins, the priest will offer us words of advice, assign us a penance, and give us absolution. The Sacrament of Reconciliation restores us to God's grace and reconciles us with the Church. It is only through this sacrament that we can be reconciled to God and the Church if we have committed a mortal sin.

Just as God in his mercy aids us spiritually, he also gives us sacramental grace to help us physically and mentally. Through the **Sacrament of Anointing of the Sick**, those who are suffering from illness are strengthened to bear their suffering, and they are united to Christ in his own suffering. The sacrament also grants the forgiveness of sins. A priest administers the Sacrament of Anointing of the Sick by anointing the forehead and hands of the sick person with the Oil of the Sick and praying for the special grace of the sacrament. Anyone who is seriously or chronically ill may receive this sacrament, especially when the person is in danger of dying.

CATECHISM Q&A

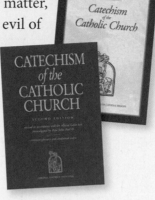

Q. What distinguishes a mortal sin?

A. There are three conditions for a sin to be a mortal sin: It is a grave matter, we have full knowledge of the evil of the act, and we commit it freely and deliberately. (See *Compendium*, Question 395; *CCC*, 1874.)

Q. Are there acts that are always immoral?

A. There are certain acts that are always morally evil and are never acceptable. For example, victimizing a weak member of society or seeking vengeance is immoral regardless of the circumstances. (See *Compendium*, Question 369; *CCC*, 1761.)

KNOW and BELIEVE

The Sacraments of Healing give us God's grace to help us in times of spiritual or physical suffering. Choose one of these two sacraments and describe how you can benefit from the grace it gives.

_____

_____

_____

_____

_____

_____

_____

_____

Calendar Connection
Sacrament of Penance

WHO Irish monks; the Pope and bishops

WHAT Introduction of frequent confession

WHERE Ireland; Rome

WHEN Seventh and thirteenth centuries

WHY In the early Church, the Sacrament of Penance was understood to be a second Baptism, to be received only once. In the seventh century, Irish monks introduced the practice of frequent penance. At the Fourth Lateran Council in 1215, the Church officially taught that every Christian should receive this sacrament at least once a year.

KNOW IT!

Sacraments of Healing
the sacraments in which we receive God's grace for the healing of our mind, body, and spirit

conscience
our ability to judge, in accordance with human reason and divine law, what is good and what is evil

SAINTLY *profiles*

As Pope, John Paul II was a model for all people of the forgiveness and mercy God offers us and of dignity in time of illness and suffering.

Blessed Pope John Paul II
1920–2005

Pope John Paul II was born Karol Wojtyla (voy-TIH-wah) in the small Polish town of Wadowice. During World War II, when the Nazis invaded Poland, Karol secretly studied for the priesthood in an underground seminary established by the archbishop of Krakow. He was ordained to the priesthood in 1946. In 1964, Father Karol was appointed archbishop of Krakow; just three years later he was made a cardinal. In 1978, Cardinal Wojtyla was elected Pope, the 264th in the Church's history. He took the name John Paul II.

From the start of his papacy, Pope John Paul II made evangelization a key part of his mission, and made pastoral visits to all parts of the world.

In 1981, a Turk named Mehmet Ali Agca shot the Pope twice in an assassination attempt and wounded him. Following Jesus' example of forgiveness and compassion for the sinner, Pope John Paul II later met with Agca in his prison cell and, gently speaking to him of the forgiveness of Christ, forgave him for what he had done.

Throughout his life, Pope John Paul II was an avid sportsman, hiking and skiing even in his sixties. In 1992, however, his health began to decline. It was later revealed that he suffered from Parkinson's disease, a degenerative disorder of the central nervous system. Near the end of his papacy, it became difficult for him to speak, and his poor health and physical suffering made public appearances difficult. Still, he bore his suffering patiently, and continued his pastoral work despite his physical pain. He entrusted his health to God, and joined his suffering with that of Christ.

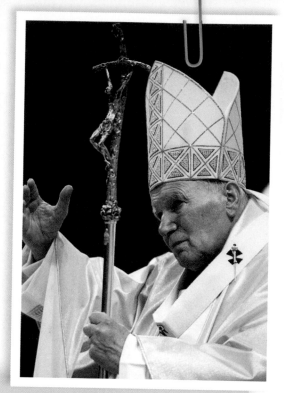

ALL ABOUT
POPE JOHN PAUL II

- ✹ First journey as Pope was to his homeland of Poland
- ✹ Established World Youth Day in 1984
- ✹ The only Polish Pope in the Church's history
- ✹ Named *Time* magazine's Person of the Year in 1994
- ✹ Died on April 2, 2005
- ✹ When he died, more than three million pilgrims came to Rome to pay their respects
- ✹ Funeral attended by presidents, prime ministers, and kings from around the world, as well as nearly two million pilgrims
- ✹ Process of making John Paul II a saint began soon after his death. He was declared "venerable" in 2009 and "blessed" in 2011.

MAKE IT HAPPEN

What does Pope John Paul II's example of forgiveness teach you about Christ's mercy? How might his endurance of his physical suffering help you turn to God when you or someone you love is seriously ill?

_____

_____

_____

_____

_____

_____

_____

_____

LET US PRAY

Act of Hope

O my God,
relying on your infinite goodness and promises,
I hope to obtain pardon of my sins,
the help of your grace,
and life everlasting,
through the merits of Jesus Christ,
my Lord and Redeemer. Amen.

KNOW IT!

Ashes

Ashes are placed on our foreheads during the Ash Wednesday liturgy to remind us of our sins and of our need of the salvation Christ won for us. The ashes are made from burnt palm branches from the preceding year's Palm Sunday.

YOUR TURN

A. Match Column A with Column B by writing the correct letter in the space provided.

A
a. conscience
b. Sacrament of Penance and Reconciliation
c. Sacrament of Anointing of the Sick
d. mortal sin
e. venial sin
f. Sacraments of Healing

B

1. _____ a conscious and free choice to do something grave against God's law, resulting in complete separation from God and his grace

2. _____ an internal sense that enables us to judge what is morally right or wrong

3. _____ the sacrament in which sins committed after Baptism are forgiven, resulting in reconciliation with God and the Church

4. _____ a less serious offense against God's will that weakens our relationship with God

5. _____ the sacraments in which we receive God's grace for the healing of our mind, body, and spirit

6. _____ the sacrament administered to the gravely ill, aging, or dying to strengthen them to bear their suffering

B. Respond to the following.

How is Pope John Paul II a model of God's forgiveness?

_____

_____

_____

Describe ways you can be more forgiving in your own life.

_____

_____

_____

Sacraments at the Service of Communion

A Prayer for Guidance

Side 1: Make known to me your ways, LORD;
teach me your paths.

Side 2: Guide me in your truth and teach me,
for you are God my savior.

All: All the paths of the LORD are
faithful love
toward those who honor
the covenant.

—Psalm 25:4, 5, 10

Live It Out

Who in your life is a model of the true meaning of married love or of service to God in the priesthood? How does this person inspire you?

BIBLE BOOST

> ## *His mother said to the servers, "Do whatever he tells you."*

The Wedding at Cana

In the Scripture story of the Wedding at Cana, we read of Jesus' first miracle, the changing of water into wine. This miracle, in which Jesus' mother intercedes on behalf of the wedding party, was the first miracle of Jesus' public **ministry**. This miracle signifies the special graces Jesus bestows on the marriage covenant.

SACRED SCRIPTURE

A reading from the holy Gospel according to John

On the third day there was a wedding in Cana in Galilee, and the mother of Jesus was there. Jesus and his disciples were also invited to the wedding. When the wine ran short, the mother of Jesus said to him, "They have no wine." [And] Jesus said to her, "Woman, how does your concern affect me? My hour has not yet come." His mother said to the servers, "Do whatever he tells you." Now there were six stone water jars there for Jewish ceremonial washings, each holding twenty to thirty gallons. Jesus told them, "Fill the jars with water." So they filled them to the brim. Then he told them, "Draw some out now and take it to the headwaiter." So they took it. And when the headwaiter tasted the water that had become wine, without knowing where it came from (although the servers who had drawn the water knew), the headwaiter called the bridegroom and said to him, "Everyone serves good wine first, and then when people have drunk freely, an inferior one; but you have kept the good wine till now." Jesus did this as the beginning of his signs in Cana in Galilee and so revealed his glory, and his disciples began to believe in him.

—John 2:1–11

The Marriage at Cana, Paolo Veronese, 1562 (oil on canvas, Venice)

START LIVING

In the story of the Wedding at Cana, we see Jesus perform his first public miracle.

What does this event tell you about Jesus' ministry?

Jesus came to the aid of the bride and groom by turning water into wine. **What are some ways that Jesus might help married couples today?**

During the Mass
The Scripture reading from the Gospel of John about the Wedding at Cana is read at Mass on the Second Sunday of Ordinary Time, during Year C. See pages 218–219.

KNOW IT!

ministry
based on a word meaning "service," a way of caring for and serving others and helping the Church fulfill its mission

OUR CATHOLIC TRADITION

Serving God Through Others

In your life, you probably know plenty of married adults—parents, aunts and uncles, family friend, and older cousins, for example. You probably also know at least one priest from your parish church. All these people are called by God to serve his Church in a special way. They are all anointed for their mission of service through the **Sacraments at the Service of Communion**. These sacraments are directed at the salvation of others.

The Sacraments at the Service of Communion are Holy Orders and Matrimony. The **Sacrament of Holy Orders** consecrates baptized men for ministry in the Church as bishops, priests, or deacons, and imprints an indelible sacramental character. Those who receive the sacrament are called ordained ministers. Through baptism we all share in the priesthood of Christ and are called to holiness, but men who receive the Sacrament of Holy Orders have different responsibilities than the **laity**. They serve the Church by teaching the faithful, leading divine worship, and governing the Church. Without ordained ministers serving as bishops, priests, or deacons, the Church would be incomplete.

Bishops receive the fullness of the Sacrament of Holy Orders. They are the visible successors of the Apostles and, with the Pope, are responsible for a group of parish communities, or a diocese. The Pope, the Bishop of Rome, is the successor of Saint Peter, the first Pope. Priests are the bishop's coworkers, and assist him by ministering to specific parishes in the diocese, preaching the Gospel, presiding at eucharistic celebrations, and administering the sacraments.

Men ordained as deacons are also called to a mission of service in the Church, but their ministry is different from that of priests. Deacons assist with the celebration of the Eucharist, including proclaiming the Gospel and giving the homily, and can baptize and bless marriages. They also serve the Church by dedicating themselves to its mission of charity.

The second Sacrament at the Service of Communion is Matrimony, or Marriage. Through the **Sacrament of Matrimony**, a baptized man and a baptized woman enter a lifelong commitment to live as faithful and loving partners. Through mutual and free consent, married people form with each other a special communion of life and love and a permanent bond that neither they nor the Church can dissolve. The object of the Sacrament of Matrimony is the good of the couple and the bringing forth and education of children. The sacrament gives spouses the grace to love each other and perfects their human love. To enter into a sacramental marriage, a couple must will to give themselves to each other mutually and wholly.

A married couple must be open to God's gift of children, and must lovingly accept them as a gift from God and provide them with a moral and spiritual education. Their home is called the "domestic church," as it is the place where children first learn about the Faith, and the virtue of Christian charity.

CATECHISM Q&A

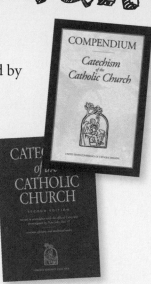

Q. How is the Sacrament of Holy Orders celebrated?

A. The Sacrament is conferred by the laying on of hands on the ordained by the bishop. With a solemn prayer of consecration, he asks God for the special outpouring of the Hoy Spirit on the man being ordained. (See *Compendium*, Question 331; *CCC*, 1597.)

Q. Who can receive the Sacrament of Holy Orders?

A. The sacrament can only be validly received by a baptized man, who must be judged suitable for the ministry by the authority of the Church. (See *Compendium*, Question 333; *CCC*, 1598.)

KNOW and BELIEVE

Who in your life is an example for you of what it means to serve the Church through one of the Sacraments at the Service of Communion?

_____

_____

_____

_____

_____

_____

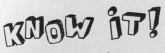

KNOW IT!

Sacraments at the Service of Communion
the sacraments that are primarily directed toward the salvation of others—namely, Holy Orders and Matrimony

In speaking about the path to sainthood, Pope John Paul II stated that "heroism must become daily, and the daily must become heroic." Saints who achieved sainthood by living out their calling to married life and as parents can be an example to us all of how the daily, or routine, can become heroic.

Saints Joachim and Anne
d. first century

Saints Joachim and Anne are the parents of the Blessed Virgin Mary. Although they were married for many years without children, they continued to pray to God that he would bless them with a child. According to tradition, an angel appeared to Anne telling her she would conceive a child and that the fruit of her womb would be blessed by the world. Many legends have developed about the lives of Joachim and Anne, but little is known with certainty. The Church honors them for their role as the parents who nurtured Mary, taught her, and helped her grow in her faith, making her worthy to be the Mother of God.

Louis and Zélie Martin
19th century

On October 19, 2008, at the Basilica of Saint Thérèse in Lisieux, France, Louis and Zélie Martin were beatified, the final step before being declared saints.

Louis and Zélie were a hardworking couple who devoted their lives to raising their daughters to be faithful to God, and were a model for them of holiness and trust in God. Their five daughters entered religious life with the Carmelites, and their daughter Thérèse, also known as the Little Flower, was declared a saint. Yet the Martins are not honored simply for raising daughters who entered religious life, nor because of Saint Thérèse's sainthood. Instead, the Church honors them for their faithfulness to God throughout their lives in the way they cared for their children, in their service to the poor, and in their deep commitment to one another. In marriage, Louis and Zélie shared a deep love and were an example of loving devotion in married life.

ALL ABOUT
SAINTS ANNE AND JOACHIM

❋ Parents of the Blessed Virgin Mary

FEAST DAY: July 26
PATRONAGE: grandparents

LOUIS AND ZÉLIE MARTIN

❋ Parents of Saint Thérèse of Lisieux

❋ All of their daughters entered religious life

❋ The first parents of a saint to be beatified

❋ The first spouses in the history of the Church to be proposed for sainthood as a couple

MAKE IT HAPPEN

Choose one pair of saints from this lesson and tell how this couple provides an example for you of how marriage is a sacrament of service to the Church and to others.

_____

_____

_____

_____

_____

_____

Catholic Social Teaching
LIFE AND DIGNITY OF THE HUMAN PERSON

Because all people are created by God for communion with him, all have intrinsic value. Sometimes we may forget that those who might seem less valuable to society—for example, the elderly, the infirm, or the poor—are also loved by God and are deserving of our love and compassion.

Reflect on ways you can live out this teaching by reaching out to those in need in your own community or in faraway places.

LET US PRAY

A Marriage Prayer

Loving Father,
we ask you to hear our prayers
and to bless all those united in Matrimony,
that we may always know of your mercy and love for us.
We ask this through Jesus Christ, our Lord. Amen.

—From the Rite of Marriage

YOUR TURN

A. Circle the letter of the correct answer.

1 The sacraments that are primarily directed toward the salvation of others are _____ .

a Baptism and Confirmation

b the Sacraments of Healing

c the Sacraments at the Service of Communion

d Holy Orders and Eucharist

2 Baptized men are ordained for permanent ministry in the Church as bishops, priests, or deacons in the Sacrament of _____ .

a Eucharist

b Anointing of the Sick

c Holy Orders

d Matrimony

3 _____ , from a word meaning "service," is a way of caring for and serving others and helping the Church fulfill its mission.

a Holy Orders

b Ministry

c Confirmation

d Matrimony

4 The sacrament by which a baptized man and a baptized woman form a lifelong covenant to love each other and care for their children is the Sacrament of _____ .

a Eucharist

b Holy Orders

c Matrimony

d Penance and Reconciliation

5 Because it is the place where children first learn about the Faith, and the virtue of Christian charity, the home of a married couple is called the _____ .

a domestic Church

b miracle at Cana

c diaconate

d ministry

6 The Sacrament of Holy Orders is conferred by _____ .

a the anointing with chrism

b the prayers of all the members of the Church

c the men being ordained

d the laying on of hands on the head of the ordained by the bishop

B. Respond to the following.

Why are Holy Orders and Matrimony sacraments of service to the Church?

_____

_____

_____

Describe ways in which someone you know lives out the calling of one of these sacraments.

_____

_____

Being Catholic

LITURGICAL PRAYER

"WHY DO I HAVE TO GO TO CHURCH?"

This can be a familiar question that children ask their parents each Sunday, perhaps because children think of Mass as too long or boring. It's easy to think this way if we expect Mass to be a form of entertainment. However, if this is our perspective, we may never understand why we have to go to church, and that doing so is about so much more than just what we see and hear. In the Mass, God leads us to our salvation as we participate in the Paschal Mystery—the Passion, death, Resurrection, and Ascension of Christ.

> "Believe what you receive and become what you believe."
> —Ordination of a Deacon

What are some feelings you experience at Mass? What are some ways you experience God's presence there?

MASS IS NOT ENTERTAINMENT

When we attend Mass, we should not have the same passive approach toward it as we would a movie or a play. At those events, it's appropriate to sit back and wait to be entertained. At Mass we are part of the assembly of those gathered in worship, sharing in the Paschal Mystery. The Mass is not just being offered by the priest, with others in the sanctuary providing backup. Instead, we are actively participating in the offering of the Mass when we sing, pray, and respond during the celebration. Therefore, we must lift our voices in prayer and in song and fully turn our hearts and minds to the presence of Christ before us.

What is one way you can participate more fully in the Mass? What is one way you can be more mindful of God's presence during Mass?

GIVING THANKS AND PRAISE TO GOD

Along with the sacrifice of the Mass, the Seven Sacraments are another important way that the Church makes Christ present to us. Three of those sacraments—Baptism, Confirmation, and Eucharist—are known as the Sacraments of Christian Initiation. We are welcomed into the life of the Church through the Sacrament of Baptism; in the Sacrament of Eucharist, we receive the Body and Blood of Jesus Christ; and the Sacrament of Confirmation strengthens the Holy Spirit in our lives. Let's take a closer look at the Sacrament of Confirmation as an example of liturgical prayer and worship in the Church.

THE RITE OF CONFIRMATION

The Rite of Confirmation traditionally takes place within the celebration of Mass, presided by the bishop, representing the Universal Church. Before the homily, the local pastor presents the candidates for Confirmation to the bishop. He explains how the candidates have prepared for the sacrament, such as by attending classes or retreats and by performing works of Christian service. The bishop then accepts the candidates for reception of the sacrament and speaks to them directly in his homily.

The rite continues with the Renewal of Baptismal Promises. Together, the candidates profess the Catholic faith in front of those gathered. They become living witnesses to the Faith by publicly proclaiming all that the Church believes and teaches. Following this, the bishop extends his hands over the candidates and invites any priests gathered to do the same. This ancient practice is known as the Laying on of Hands.

After the Laying on of Hands, each candidate comes forward with his or her sponsor and is anointed with Sacred Chrism. Calling each candidate by his or her Confirmation name, the bishop says, "Be sealed with the gift of the Holy Spirit." Each candidate responds, "Amen." This anointing symbolizes how each of the confirmed is set apart to do the work of Christ. The Mass then continues as usual with the Prayer of the Faithful followed by the Liturgy of the Eucharist.

Through the Mass and other sacraments, we become active participants in the liturgical life of the Church. In the words of Pope Benedict XVI,

"Whenever you gather for Mass, when you go to confession, whenever you celebrate any of the Sacraments, Jesus is at work."

What can you do to make Mass and other forms of liturgical prayer a more important part of your life?

Living

UNIT 3

The Christian Life

The Word of God is a light for our path. We must assimilate it in faith and prayer and put it into practice. (CCC, 1802)

The Ten Commandments

1. I am the Lord your God. You shall not have other gods besides me.

2. You shall not take the name of the Lord, your God, in vain.

3. Remember to keep holy the Sabbath day.

4. Honor your father and mother.

5. You shall not kill.

6. You shall not commit adultery.

7. You shall not steal.

8. You shall not bear false witness against your neighbor.

9. You shall not covet your neighbor's wife.

10. You shall not covet anything that belongs to your neighbor.

Created in God's Image

A Psalm Prayer

How varied are your works, LORD!
   In wisdom you have wrought them all;
   the earth is full of your creatures.
When you send forth your breath, they are created,
   and you renew the face of the earth.

—Psalm 104:24, 30

Live It Out
Do you see the image of God in yourself? In what ways do you fall short? What improvements can you make?

> *God looked at everything he had made, and he found it very good.*

God Creates Humankind in His Own Image

In the Book of Genesis, we can find two stories of Creation. In the following passage, from the First Story of Creation, we learn that when God created the universe and all forms of life, he set us apart by making us in his own image. This means that while the rest of creation simply has a physical form, we are both physical and spiritual beings.

SACRED SCRIPTURE

A READING FROM THE BOOK OF GENESIS

In the beginning, when God created the heavens and the earth, God said: "Let us make man in our image, after our likeness. Let them have dominion over the fish of the sea, the birds of the air, and the cattle, and over all the wild animals and all the creatures that crawl on the ground."

God created man in his image;
in the image of God he created him;
male and female he created them.

God blessed them, saying: "Be fertile and multiply; fill the earth and subdue it. Have dominion over the fish of the sea, the birds of the air, and all the living things that move on the earth." God also said: "See, I give you every seed-bearing plant all over the earth and every tree that has seed-bearing fruit on it to be your food; and to all the animals of the land, all the birds of the air, and all the living creatures that crawl on the ground, I give all the green plants for food." And so it happened. God looked at everything he had made, and he found it very good.

—Genesis 1:1, 26–31

START LIVING

In the Story of Creation in the Book of Genesis, we read that God looked approvingly on all that he had created, and found it to be very good.

How can this view help you in the way you look upon and treat others?

_____

_____

_____

_____

How can it influence the way you see yourself and take care of your physical, spiritual, and emotional well-being?

_____

_____

_____

_____

_____

_____

Stop and Think

Choose a phrase from the Scripture reading that can influence how you value human life. What is its message for you?

_____

_____

_____

OUR CATHOLIC TRADITION

See what love the Father has bestowed on us that we may be called the children of God.
—1 John 3:1

Created in the Likeness of God

In the modern world, there is much emphasis on material things. This focus on material value often influences how we see ourselves and other people. For example, we often judge ourselves and others by such factors as how we look, the clothes we wear, and how much money we have. By focusing on such external elements, we overlook a significant aspect of who we are, and of our purpose in life.

In the Book of Genesis we read the Story of Creation, which is described in figurative language and is authentically interpreted by the Church in the light of the New Testament and Tradition. The Bible expresses the reality of creation in symbolic language and emphasizes that God alone created the universe freely with wisdom and love. Unlike a scientific explanation that strives to provide precise details of a particular phenomenon, the Story of Creation is more concerned with the big picture—that God created the world and humankind. More important, the Book of Genesis tells us that among all his creation, God set us apart by creating us in his image and likeness— spiritual beings with a body and a soul, and a natural longing to live in communion with him. From the moment we are first formed we exist as a unity of body and **soul**. The soul is immortal, meaning that it does not perish when separated from the body at death. It will be reunited with the body at the final resurrection.

In the Story of Creation we also read that God created humans as social beings. After creating Adam, God said, "It is not good for the man to be alone. I will make a suitable partner for him" (Genesis 2:18). Thus God created Eve. This partnership between man and woman has always been the primary form of communion between persons. Through this communion, men and women follow God's command to Adam and Eve: "Be fertile and multiply; fill the earth and subdue it. Have dominion over … all the living things that fill the earth" (Genesis 1:28). For married couples, responding to this command means accepting God's invitation to have children and to raise them to know and love God. For all people, it is a call to **stewardship** of creation, a responsibility to protect and care for all the good God has created, and to use it for the good of all people rather than as our own possession intended to do with as we please.

CATECHISM Q&A

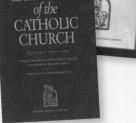

Q. Why do we have a desire for God?

A. God created people in his own image, and imprinted on their heart the desire for union with him. Even if we ignore this desire, God never ceases to draw us to himself. (See *Compendium*, Question 2; *CCC*, 44–45.)

Q. Where does the soul come from?

A. The spiritual soul is created by God at the moment of our conception. It does not perish when it is separated from the body in death and it will once again be reunited with the body at the final resurrection. (See *Compendium*, Question 70; *CCC*, 382.)

Q. What relationship has God established between man and woman?

A. God created man and woman with equal dignity. At the same time, they are created to complement, or balance, one another. God created them for one another to form a communion and to transmit human life. (See *Compendium*, Question 71; *CCC*, 383.)

KNOW and BELIEVE

God created each of us in his own image; therefore, our value as individuals goes far beyond what is physical and visible to ourselves and others. How can knowing this help you when you are feeling dissatisfied with something about yourself?

_____

_____

_____

_____

Calendar Connection
Humanae Vitae

WHO Pope Paul VI

WHAT *Humanae Vitae* ("Of Human Life")

WHERE From the Vatican

WHEN 1968

WHY To reaffirm the Church's prohibition on artificial contraception and its stance against abortion, and address other issues pertaining to human life. The teachings in Pope Paul VI's encyclical *Humanae Vitae* have been clearly reaffirmed by both Pope John Paul II and Pope Benedict XVI.

KNOW iT!

soul
the invisible or spiritual part of a person that is immortal and will live on after death in Heaven, Hell, or Purgatory

stewardship
the responsibility to care for and protect the gifts of creation that God has given us

SAINTLY *profiles*

Recognizing that we are created in God's image means that we respect ourselves and appreciate the goodness God has given us. It also means that we must see God in others, and accept that as children of the same Creator, all people are our brothers and sisters and must be treated with compassion and dignity. Saint Martin de Porres is a model of living out this belief.

Saint Martin de Porres 1597–1639

Martin de Porres was born in Lima, Peru. He was the illegitimate son of a freed woman from Panama, of African or Native American origin, and a Spanish nobleman from Lima. Martin was often treated cruelly because of his mixed race and social status.

At age twelve, Martin became an apprentice to a barber-surgeon, a commonly combined profession in those times. He learned basic medical care, such as drawing blood, tending to wounds, and administering medicines. At age fifteen, Martin was taken in by the Dominicans as a servant. He later became a Dominican brother.

Martin lived a life of penance that included frequent fasting. He dedicated his life to serving the poor. He established an orphanage and a children's hospital in Lima, and tended to slaves arriving on ships from Africa. Martin saw Christ in all people and reached out with love and compassion to all who were suffering or in need. When an epidemic struck Lima, Martin worked tirelessly to serve the sick, tending to their needs and transporting many to a local convent where they could be cared for.

During Martin's lifetime many miracles were attributed to him, including the ability to miraculously appear beside those who were sick and suffering in faraway places. An African slave who had been in irons aboard a slave ship said he had been visited by Martin, who came to relieve and console many like himself on the ship, telling them of Heaven. The same slave later learned that Martin had never left Lima.

ALL ABOUT
SAINT MARTIN DE PORRES

* Saw the image of God in all people
* Miraculously able to distribute large sums of money to the poor each week
* It is said he so loved all of God's creatures that he even refused to chase away or hurt the mice that came into the friary
* Close friend of Saint Rose of Lima, also from Peru
* Thousands turned out to pay their respects when he died
* Canonized in 1962

FEAST DAY: November 3

MAKE IT HAPPEN

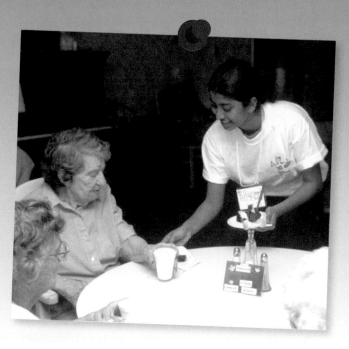

In what ways did Saint Martin de Porres demonstrate that he saw the image of God in all people?

_____

_____

_____

_____

Describe two simple ways that you can follow Saint Martin's example in your life.

_____

_____

_____

_____

_____

KNOW iT!

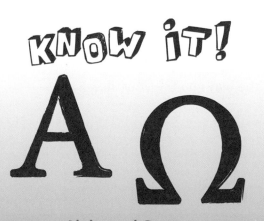

Alpha and Omega
The alpha and omega are the first and last letters of the Greek alphabet. In the Book of Revelation, the last book of the New Testament, Jesus calls himself the Alpha and the Omega, signifying his eternal nature.

LET US PRAY

A Prayer of Praise
Lord, you have given everything its place in the world, and no one can make it otherwise. For it is your creation, the heavens and the earth and the stars: you are Lord of all.
—Esther 13:9, 10–11

YOUR TURN

A. Complete the following sentences.

1 God created us in his own image, which means that unlike the rest of creation, we are both physical and _____ beings.

2 The invisible or spiritual part of a person that is immortal and will live on after death in Heaven, Hell, or Purgatory is the _____ .

3 The spiritual soul is created by God at the moment of our _____ .

4 _____ is the responsibility to care for and protect the gifts of Creation that God has given us.

5 For _____ , responding to God's command to be fertile and multiply means accepting God's invitation to have children and to raise them to know and love him.

6 Saint Martin de Porres saw _____ in all people and is an example to us of how we must treat others.

B. Respond to the following.
When God created all living things, how did he make us different from all other created beings?

_____

_____

_____

What are some ways you can reflect God's image in the way you live your life?

_____

_____

_____

The Fall of Man and the Gift of God's Grace

A Blessing Prayer

All: Bless the LORD, my soul;
all my being, bless his holy name!

Side 1: The LORD does righteous deeds,
brings justice to all the oppressed.

All: Bless the LORD, my soul;
all my being, bless his holy name!

Side 2: Merciful and gracious is the LORD,
slow to anger, abounding in kindness.

All: Bless the LORD, my soul;
all my being, bless his holy name!

—Psalm 103:1, 6, 8

Live It Out

How does knowing that God is loving and merciful help you when you fall short in following his will?

BIBLE BOOST

> *The LORD God formed man out of the clay of the ground and blew into his nostrils the breath of life, and so man became a living being.*

The Fall of Adam and Eve

When God created Adam and Eve, he placed them in the Garden of Eden, in a state of happiness and friendship with him. But through the exercise of their **free will**, and their choice to disobey God, Adam and Eve committed the first sin and lost their original state of perfect holiness and justice, not only for themselves, but for all human beings.

SACRED SCRIPTURE

A READING FROM THE BOOK OF GENESIS

The LORD God formed man out of the clay of the ground and blew into his nostrils the breath of life, and so man became a living being.

Then the LORD God planted a garden in Eden, in the east, and placed there the man whom he had formed. Out of the ground the LORD God made various trees grow that were delightful to look at and good for food, with the tree of life in the middle of the garden and the tree of the knowledge of good and bad.

Now the serpent was the most cunning of all the animals the LORD God had made. The serpent asked the woman, "Did God really tell you not to eat from any of the trees in the garden?" The woman answered the serpent: "We may eat of the fruit of the trees in the garden; it is only about the fruit of the tree in the middle of the garden that God said, 'You shall not eat it or even touch it, lest you die.'" But the serpent said to the woman: "You certainly will not die! No, God knows well that the moment you eat of it your eyes will be opened and you will be like gods who know what is good and what is bad." The woman saw that the tree was good for food, pleasing to the eyes, and desirable for gaining wisdom. So she took some of its fruit and ate it; and she also gave some to her husband, who was with her, and he ate it. Then the eyes of both of them were opened, and they realized that they were naked; so they sewed fig leaves together and made loincloths for themselves.

—Genesis 2:7–9; 3:1–7

START LIVING

Because of the serpent's temptation, Adam and Eve disobeyed God and put themselves ahead of him. Are there times when others, such as friends, classmates, or even celebrities, convince you to do something that your conscience tells you is wrong?

What can you do to be stronger in the face of such temptation?

Rather than finding great satisfaction after taking of the forbidden fruit, Adam and Eve instead felt shame at their nakedness. **How can this realization guide you in resisting temptation?**

During the Mass
The Story of the Fall of Adam and Eve from the Book of Genesis is read at Mass on the first Sunday of Lent, during Year A. See pages 218-219.

KNOW iT!

free will
the freedom God gives us to choose between good and evil

OUR CATHOLIC TRADITION

The Fall from Grace

The story of Adam and Eve's fall from the Garden of Eden explains much about human nature and about the struggle we all face in resisting temptation and following God's law. That is because when Adam and Eve disobeyed God, their sin affected not only them, but all humankind, and weakened human nature,

> Now that you have been freed from sin and have become slaves of God, the benefit that you have leads to sanctification, and its end is eternal life.
> —Romans 6:22

Adam and Eve, The Temptation and Expulsion, Michelangelo Buonarotti, c. 1510 (fresco, Sistine Chapel)

making it prone to sin. They transmitted to all of us a human nature deprived of original holiness. This deprivation is called Original Sin, and because of it we are weakened in our power to resist sin.

The Story of the Fall also teaches us another important fact about our relationship with God: Just as God gave Adam and Eve the freedom to choose whether to obey him, he gives us the freedom to choose between good and sin and makes us responsible for our own actions. There are times when the circumstances can affect our moral responsibility, such as when we are acting out of ignorance or fear. Ignorance, however, does not automatically excuse our wrong actions, because we have an obligation to learn God's law and his will.

To best live a moral life, we have to strengthen the **virtues** God has given us. Virtue is a disposition to do good, and governs our actions and guides our conduct. There are two kinds of Virtues: Cardinal Virtues and Theological Virtues. The Cardinal Virtues, also called human or moral virtues, are Prudence, Justice, Fortitude, and Temperance. These virtues are part of the human intellect and will and develop through deliberate effort. The Theological Virtues are Faith, Hope, and Charity. They help us to live in a relationship with the Holy Trinity.

Because human nature is susceptible to sin, it is important and reassuring for us to know that God is merciful. We first experience God's mercy and forgiveness in the Sacrament of Baptism, when the **grace** of the Holy Spirit pardons us from sin and unites us with Christ. The Sacrament of Penance is another source of forgiveness. Through these sacraments, the Holy Spirit gives us **sanctifying grace** to heal us of sin and make us holy. The grace of the Holy Spirit enables us to turn back to God when we sin, and to experience forgiveness and **justification**, or being brought back into a right relationship with God through the forgiveness of our sins and a renewal of our holiness.

CATECHISM Q&A

Q. What are the human virtues?

A. The human virtues, also called the Cardinal Virtues, are perfections of our intellect and will that govern our actions, order our passions and guide our conduct according to reason and faith. We acquire and strengthen them by the repetition of morally good acts. (See *Compendium*, Question 378; *CCC*, 1834, 1839.)

Q. What goods and graces can we merit for ourselves and others?

A. Moved by the Holy Spirit, we can merit for ourselves and for others the graces needed for sanctification and for attaining eternal life. Even earthly goods can be merited in accordance with God's plan. (See *Compendium*, Question 427; *CCC*, 2027.)

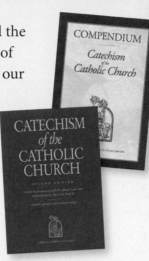

CATHOLIC CUSTOMS
INDULGENCES

An indulgence is the reduction of punishment for sin. We can receive indulgences because of the merits of Christ, his Blessed Mother, or the saints. One common way to gain an indulgence is to participate in certain devotional practices, such as praying the Rosary. An indulgence may be plenary, meaning it takes away all punishment for sin, or partial. We may gain indulgences for ourselves or for the souls in purgatory.

KNOW and BELIEVE

Developing the Virtues within ourselves strengthens us to do good and to avoid sin. Describe a situation when you chose to do the morally right thing even though it was difficult, then tell how this experience strengthened you to resist temptation on another occasion.

_____

_____

_____

_____

KNOW IT!

grace
God's loving presence in our lives, given to us freely, to perfect our human freedom

virtue
a disposition to do good that directs our actions and guides our conduct

sanctifying grace
a gift of God infused by the Holy Spirit into the soul, by which we are made holy and restored to friendship with God

SAINTLY *profiles*

As a young man, Saint Augustine often made choices that were not pleasing to God, but with the guidance of of holy people around him, he came to understand that the happiness and wisdom he had been searching for can only be found in God. Through his personal experience and his writings, Saint Augustine teaches us much about sin and conversion.

Saint Augustine 354–430

Saint Augustine is one of the most important figures in the development of Western Christianity, but before becoming such a leading figure in the Church, he lived a very different life. Augustine was born in North Africa, in present-day Algeria. He was the son of a devoutly Christian mother and a wealthy merchant who rejected Christianity. Despite his mother's persistent pleas, Augustine refused to accept the Christian faith, and instead lived a self-indulgent and sinful lifestyle. In his late twenties, Augustine traveled to Rome and then to Milan to serve as a professor of rhetoric.

Augustine's mother, Monica, traveled with him, and continued to pray for her son's conversion. Although Monica's prayers and influence had made Augustine more open to Christianity, it was the Bishop of Milan, Ambrose, who had the greatest effect on Augustine. Through Ambrose's teachings, Augustine came to recognize that his search for happiness through earthly pleasures was in truth a search for God. He was baptized by Ambrose in 387. He abandoned his teaching position in Milan, and devoted himself entirely to serving God. He was ordained a priest in 391, in Hippo, in North Africa, and later became that city's bishop.

After his conversion to Christianity, Augustine became one of the leading thinkers of the early Church and an ardent defender of Christianity. His extensive writings have had a profound influence on Christian thought. Along with clarifying the theology of Original Sin, Augustine also developed the concept of the just war, war that is acceptable because of certain conditions—such as provocation through aggression. This principle still guides the modern view of the morality of war.

ALL ABOUT
SAINT AUGUSTINE

- Baptized on Easter Sunday, at around age thirty-three
- Autobiography, *Confessions*, tells of Augustine's struggle with good and evil, of his conversion, and of the role of grace in his life
- Honored as a Father of the Church and a Doctor of the Church
- Mother, Monica, also a saint

FEAST DAY: August 28

MAKE IT HAPPEN

Saint Augustine is one of the Church's greatest saints, yet he did not always lead a saintly life.

What does his story teach you about following your own path to holiness and about God's mercy?

_____

_____

_____

_____

_____

_____

_____

Catholic Social Teaching
SOLIDARITY

All people—rich and poor, young and old, weak and strong—have equal dignity and rights that flow from that dignity. As part of one human family, we are all dependent on one another and responsible for one another, and must work to reduce social inequalities and provide for one another's needs.

Think about ways that you can show more responsibility for other members of society, especially those who are in need, and make this attitude of solidarity a part of your life.

LET US PRAY

The Confiteor

*I confess to almighty God
and to you, my brothers and sisters,
that I have greatly sinned,
in my thoughts and in my words,
in what I have done
and in what I have failed to do,
through my fault, through my fault,
through my most grievous fault;
therefore I ask blessed Mary ever-Virgin,
all the Angels and Saints,
and you, my brothers and sisters,
to pray for me to the Lord our God.*

—**Roman Missal**

YOUR TURN

A. Match Column A with Column B by writing the letter of the correct answer in the space provided.

A	B
a. free will	**1.** _____ being brought back into a right relationship with God through the forgiveness of our sins and a renewal of our holiness
b. virtue	**2.** _____ the freedom God gives us to choose between good and evil
c. sanctifying grace	**3.** _____ Faith, Hope, and Charity
d. justification	**4.** _____ Prudence, Justice, Fortitude, and Temperance
e. Theological Virtues	**5.** _____ a gift of God by which we are made holy and restored to friendship with God
f. Cardinal Virtues	**6.** _____ a disposition to do good that directs our actions and guides our conduct

B. Respond to the following.

What does the Story of the Fall of Adam and Eve teach us about our own ability to resist temptation and sin?

_____

_____

_____

Reflect on an occasion when you had difficulty avoiding temptation but succeeded in doing so. How did that strengthen you to resist temptation at other times?

_____

_____

_____

_____

_____

The Church as Mother and Teacher

Prayer for the Church

Almighty ever-living God,
by whose Spirit the whole body of the Church
is sanctified and governed,
hear our humble prayer for your ministers,
that, by the gift of your grace,
all may serve you faithfully.
Through Christ our Lord.
Amen.

—From the Prayer of the Faithful,
Good Friday of the Lord's Passion, *Roman Missal*

Live It Out
Do you think of yourself only as an individual follower of Jesus, or do you also see yourself as an important part of the Catholic Church?

BIBLE BOOST

> *"For where two or three are gathered in my name, there am I in the midst of them."*

Jesus Gives Authority to the Church

In the following Scripture passage, Jesus speaks of how sinners are to be admonished, and tells his disciples that the rules they establish will become the rules of his Kingdom. In living a moral life as followers of Jesus Christ, we are guided by the Church, to whom, through the disciples, Jesus gave the authority to act as mother and teacher to all the faithful.

SACRED SCRIPTURE

A READING FROM THE HOLY GOSPEL ACCORDING TO MATTHEW

[Jesus said to his disciples:] "If your brother sins against you, go and tell him his fault between you and him alone. If he listens to you, you have won over your brother. If he does not listen, take one or two others along with you, so that 'every fact may be established on the testimony of two or three witnesses.' If he refuses to listen to them, tell the church. If he refuses to listen even to the church, then treat him as you would a Gentile or a tax collector. Again, amen, I say to you, whatever you bind on earth shall be bound in heaven, and whatever you loose on earth shall be loosed in heaven. Again, [amen], I say to you, if two of you agree on earth about anything for which they are to pray, it shall be granted to them by my heavenly Father. For where two or three are gathered together in my name, there am I in the midst of them."

—Matthew 18:15–20

START LIVING

In the Scripture reading about the brother who sins, Jesus says that we first must tell the sinner his fault privately. He then says that if the sinner does not listen, we must try again, with the help of others.

What does this message tell you about your personal responsibility to guide others in making moral choices?

This message tells me to make those who sins aware of what they have done, as well as privately speak to them and talk about what they have done.

Describe a situation when you might thoughtfully guide another person to realize he or she has done wrong. Tell what advice you might provide about making a morally good choice instead.

If someone has said a rude comment, bring them to a private place and describe what they said and what it did.

Stop and Think

Jesus said, "Where two or three are gathered together in my name, there am I in the midst of them" (Matthew 18:20). What are some occasions when you are part of a group gathered in Jesus' name?

OUR CATHOLIC TRADITION

> "I am the vine, you are the branches. Whoever remains in me and I in him will bear much fruit."
> —John 15:5

The Church, Mother and Teacher

As a young child, you were taught right and wrong by family members—parents, grandparents, siblings, or other relatives. When you went to school, you quickly learned that there, too, were rules you had to follow. Society also has a lot of rules and laws about how we are to conduct ourselves. But along with all of the rules that are imposed by others, you also have your conscience—a natural ability to know the difference between right and wrong, good and evil. However, our natural ability to judge between good and sin is not always sound, and throughout our lives we need moral guidance to help us know what God truly approves of.

Along with the guidance we receive from others, moral guidance comes to us through the Word of God, the Scriptures, and through the teachings of the Church. In the Scriptures we learn what it means to live as God's people. The Old Testament presents us with the Law of Moses, or the **Old Law**, as it was given to the Israelites. The Old Law is summed up in the Ten Commandments, and is a preparation for the Gospel. In the New Testament we learn the **New Law**, Jesus' teachings about how to live as Christians. The New Law is most clearly expressed in the Sermon on the Mount. (See Matthew 5—7.) Through the Church's teachings, we learn what all that the Scriptures say means for our lives today.

Jesus entrusted the Church with the mission of bringing his message of salvation to all people. One way the Church does this is by providing us with moral guidance, starting with its example of charity and justice in the world. The Church is the Temple of the Holy Spirit. Guided by the Holy Spirit, she provides us with teachings that can lead us to a moral life and to eternal salvation. Living a moral life, making choices that are pleasing to God and avoiding sin, is a form of spiritual worship. We are nourished to live a moral life by the liturgy and the Sacraments.

The Church's moral teachings begin with the direction given by Christ's two Commandments of Love: to love God with all our hearts and our neighbors as ourselves. (See Matthew 22:37–40.) Love is the essential foundation of the moral life. At the same time, rules and laws are needed to see how to apply love in our relationships, and these come to us through the Sermon on the Mount, the Ten Commandments, the **Precepts of the Church**, and all of the Church's teachings. The Precepts of the Church call us to live a moral life bound to and nourished by the Liturgy and the celebration of the sacraments. **(See page 205 for more on the Precepts of the Church.)**

CATECHISM Q&A

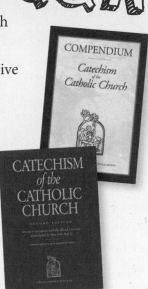

Q. How does the Church nourish the moral life of a Christian?

A. Through the Church, we receive the Word of God, the teachings of God's law, and the grace of the Sacraments. United with the sacrifice of Christ in the Sacrament of the Eucharist, our moral lives become an act of worship. (See *Compendium*, Question 429; *CCC*, 2047–2048.)

Q. Why does the Magisterium speak out on moral issues?

A. It is the duty of the Magisterium, the teaching office of the Church, to preach the Faith and to instruct the faithful in how to put it into practice. This duty extends to specific principles of how we are to live, because their observance is necessary for salvation. (See *Compendium*, Question 430; *CCC*, 2049–2050.)

Calendar Connection
First U.S. Bishop

WHO John Carroll

WHAT Appointed first U.S. Bishop

WHERE Baltimore, Maryland

WHEN 1789

WHY John Carroll was the first Catholic bishop appointed in the United States. He greatly influenced the growth of the Church in America. He encouraged the building of new churches, helped to create what is today Georgetown University, established seminaries for the training of priests, and encouraged religious orders to establish convents and schools.

KNOW and BELIEVE

Choose one of the Precepts of the Church and reflect on how well you live it. Then describe how you can follow it more fully.

One precept I live by is receiving Communion once a week during the Easter Season. I can improve by going to church more often and never missing a week.

KNOW IT!

Old Law
the Law of Moses, the Ten Commandments

New Law
the law of love taught by Jesus in the Gospels and fulfilled in his life, death, and Resurrection; the perfection of God's law

Precepts of the Church
obligations established by the Church that all Catholics must observe

SAINTLY *profiles*

Pope John XXIII believed that the Church needed renewal to enable it to minister more effectively to the modern world. He brought about this renewal by calling for the Second Vatican Council (1962–1965). The Council had a profound effect on the Church and its interaction with contemporary society, and its view of its place in the modern world.

Blessed Pope John XXIII 1881–1963

Pope John XXIII was born Angelo Guiseppe Roncalli to a peasant family in northern Italy. He was ordained to the priesthood in 1904. He served as a stretcher-bearer and chaplain in the Italian army during World War I. He later held a number of important positions in the Church, including that of bishop. In 1953 he was raised to the rank of cardinal by Pope Pius XII. Upon the death of Pius XII in 1958, Cardinal Roncalli was elected Pope, taking the name John XXIII.

Because of his advanced age, many thought John XXIII's papacy would be short and would bring about few, if any, important changes. Although his papacy was short, only five years, it led to some of the greatest changes the Church had seen for centuries. Within just three months of becoming Pope, John XXIII had called for a worldwide **ecumenical council**, a gathering of bishops from around the world called together by the Pope or approved by him. This ecumenical council became known as Vatican Council II. Among his goals for the Council were to discover more effective ways to teach the Faith, to deepen the understanding of the Church's doctrine, and to seek unity within the Church and with Christians separated from Catholicism. The Second Vatican Council is often noted as the start of a new era in the life of the Church. Pope John XXIII died less than a year after the start of Vatican II, but his vision set the tone for the whole Council.

Pope John XXIII's contributions to the Church also include a number of encyclicals, or letters to the whole Church, that reflected his view of the Church's place in the modern world. Among these was *Pacem in terris* ("Peace on Earth"), which was addressed to the whole world, rather than just to Catholics. In it Pope John XXIII stated that conflict among nations should be resolved through negotiation and mutual understanding, not through warfare.

ALL ABOUT
POPE JOHN XXIII

- Nearly 80 years old when elected Pope

- Called for Vatican Council II to bring about renewal in the Church

- Posthumously awarded the Presidential Medal of Freedom, the United States' highest civilian award, by President Lyndon B. Johnson

- Beatified: September 3, 2000

FEAST DAY: October 11, the date of the opening of the Second Vatican Council

MAKE IT HAPPEN

One way Pope John XXIII strengthened the Church was by reaching out to all Catholics as well as to those who had separated from the Church.

How can you work to strengthen the Church among people you know?

_____

_____

_____

In _Pacem in terris_, John XXIII said that conflict should be resolved through peaceful means, not war. How can you apply that message to your own life?

_____

_____

_____

IHS

This monogram consists of the Greek letters _iota_ (I), _eta_ (H), and _sigma_ (S), the first three letters of Jesus' name in Greek. The letters are also used to spell out the Latin phrase _"Iesous Hominum Salvator"_ ("Jesus, Savior of man").

LET US PRAY

A Prayer of Consecration
May the God of peace, who brought up from the dead the great shepherd of the sheep, Jesus Christ our Lord, furnish us with all that is good, that we may do his will. May he carry out in us what is pleasing to him through Jesus Christ, to whom be glory forever and ever. Amen.

—Based on Hebrews 13:20–21

YOUR TURN

A. Circle the letter of the correct answer.

1 Jesus gave _____ the authority to act as mother and teacher to all the faithful.

a the disciples   c the Pope

b the Church   d the Magisterium

130

2 The Law of Moses, or the Ten Commandments, is called _____ .

a the New Law

b the Precepts of the Church

c the Old Law

d Infallibility   *132*

3 The Sermon on the Mount, the Ten Commandments, the Precepts of the Church, and all of the Church's teachings are sources of _____ .

a civil law   *132*

b the sacramental life of the Church

c moral guidance for us

d sacrifices we can make

4 The _____ is the law of love taught by Jesus in the Gospels.

a New Law   c Old Law

b encyclical   d catechism

132

5 The basic obligations established by the Church that all Catholics must observe are called the _____ .

a Precepts of the Church

b New Law

c Old Law   *132*

d Magisterium

6 An ecumenical council is _____ .

134

a the moral guidance we receive from the Church

b the development of the Church's teachings to meet the needs of a changing world

c an encyclical issued by the Pope

d a gathering of bishops from around the world called together by the Pope or approved by him

B. Respond to the following.   *132-133*

In what ways does the Church provide moral guidance for us and nourish us to live a moral life?

_____

_____

Describe a time when a young person your age can follow the Church's teachings in making a moral choice.

_____

_____

_____

The Ten Commandments: Love the Lord Your God

A Prayer of Praise

Happy those whose way is blameless,
who walk by the teaching of the LORD.
Happy those who observe God's decrees,
who seek the LORD with all their
heart.
They do no wrong;
they walk in God's ways.
May my ways be firm
in the observance of your laws.
In your laws I take delight;
I will never forget your word.

—Psalm 119:1–3, 5, 16

Live It Out
Do you know each of the Ten Commandments? How can knowing the Commandments help you live a better and more moral life?

BIBLE BOOST

> *"I, the LORD, am your God, who brought you out of the land of Egypt, that place of slavery."*

The Ten Commandments

When God led the Israelites out of slavery in Egypt, they traveled for three months in the desert, led by Moses. God promised them that they would be his chosen people if they kept their covenant with him. To guide them in doing so, he gave them the Ten Commandments. In the same way, these Commandments guide us in being faithful to God and his will.

SACRED SCRIPTURE

A reading from the Book of Exodus

In those days, God delivered all these commandments:
"I, the LORD, am your God, who brought you out of the land of Egypt, that place of slavery. You shall not have other gods besides me.

"You shall not take the name of the LORD, your God, in vain. For the LORD will not leave unpunished him who takes his name in vain.

"Remember to keep holy the sabbath day.

"Honor your father and your mother, that you may have a long life in the land which the LORD, your God, is giving you.

"You shall not kill.

"You shall not commit adultery.

"You shall not steal.

"You shall not bear false witness against your neighbor.

"You shall not covet your neighbor's house. You shall not covet your neighbor's wife, nor his male or female slave, nor his ox or ass, nor anything else that belongs to him."

—Exodus 20:1–3, 7–8, 12–17

START LIVING

The Israelites' false gods took the form of carved idols and a golden calf.

What are false idols that exist in the world today? How can you keep these from becoming false gods in your own life so that you may truly worship only God?

Who in your life is a model for you in how to honor and worship God? What does this person teach you about what it means to follow the Commandments?

During the Mass
The Book of Exodus passage containing the Ten Commandments is the First Reading at Mass on the Third Sunday of Lent, during Year B. See pages 218-219.

OUR CATHOLIC TRADITION

Commandments 1–3: Love of God

How well do you know the Ten Commandments? You've probably seen images of the stone tablets containing the Commandments, or artwork of Moses holding those stone tablets up high for the Israelites to see. But do you know each of the Commandments and what it means for how you are to live your life today?

When God gave the Ten Commandments to the Israelites through Moses, he established a covenant with all people and revealed his law for all generations. We are able to understand by human reason God's truth as it is expressed in the Ten Commandments because the Commandments are an expression of the natural law that is implanted in our hearts. The **natural law** expresses the dignity of all people, created in God's image, and guides our understanding of our rights and responsibilities. The natural law remains the same throughout time, and provides the basis not only of moral rules but also of civil law.

By giving us the Ten Commandments, God gave us clear rules that help us understand the natural law and how it must guide all aspects of our lives. Even when their requirements appear challenging, we are assured that God will give us the grace we need to obey them.

The first three Commandments concern our relationship with and love for God, while the next seven are concerned with love of neighbor. In this lesson we examine the first three Commandments and what obeying each of them means.

1 I am the Lord your God: you shall not have strange gods before me.

- Believe in God, love him, and hope in him above all else, and offer him the worship that is his due.
- Trust in God alone, acknowledging him as our Creator and Savior.
- Superstition and astrology violate the First Commandment.
- **Atheism**, or denial of the existence of God, is a sin against the First Commandment.

2 You shall not take the name of the Lord your God in vain.

- The name of God is holy and must be spoken with respect.
- **Blasphemy**, or using the name of God, Jesus Christ, Mary, or the saints in an offensive way, is a violation of the Second Commandment.

3 Remember to keep holy the Lord's Day.

- Sunday, or the Lord's Day, celebrates the day of Christ's Resurrection, and is the foremost Holy Day of Obligation. We are required to participate in the celebration of Mass on Sundays and other Holy Days of Obligation. **(See page 209 for a list of the Holy Days of Obligation.)**
- Honor God by participating in prayer, refraining from unnecessary work, spending time with family, serving the elderly or the sick, and engaging in activities that refresh your mind and body.

CATECHISM Q&A

Q. Does the First Commandment forbid the veneration, or reverence, of sacred images, such as statues or other artwork of Jesus or Mary and the saints?

A. The Christian veneration of sacred images is justified by the Incarnation, the Son of God becoming man, in whom God is made visible. However, this does not mean we adore the image; rather, it means we adore the one who is represented by the image. (See *Compendium*, Question 446; *CCC*, 2141.)

Q. Why is a false oath forbidden?

A. Perjury, or making a false oath, is forbidden because it calls upon God to be witness to a lie. It is a grave offense against God, who is always faithful to his promises. (See *Compendium*, Questions 448, 449; *CCC*, 2163.)

CATHOLIC CUSTOMS
ICONS

An icon is a religious work of art, usually a painting, typically featuring Jesus, the Blessed Mother, or a saint. Icons are most often painted on a flat wood panel, and typically combine striking imagery with vivid colors. They are venerated as sacred images. Icons are a central feature in Greek Orthodox churches and Eastern Rite Catholic churches.

KNOW IT!

natural law
our God-given understanding of the created moral order that forms the basis of personal morality and civil norms

KNOW and BELIEVE

Name at least two things you can you do to better keep the Third Commandment.

SAINTLY *profiles*

The first three Commandments instruct us in how we are to love God. For most of us, our love for God does not entail any unbearable sacrifices, but instead requires everyday acts of holiness and faithfulness to God's laws. For some, however, love of God and faithfulness to his Church has meant sacrificing their lives as **martyrs**. Saint Andrew Kim, along with many other Korean Catholics, was true to God and his faith even when it meant he would be persecuted and killed for it.

Saint Andrew Kim Taegon 1821–1846

Christianity came to Korea during the Japanese invasion in 1592, most likely brought by Christian Japanese soldiers. Because Korea refused almost any contact with the outside world, evangelization was difficult. However, around 1777, Christian literature obtained from Jesuits in China made its way into Korea, and the number of Koreans who learned about Christianity grew. This group of Korean Catholics formed a home church and met in secret, to avoid persecution, and without any priests to celebrate the Sacraments. Religious freedom did not come to Korea until 1883; until then, Christians could be sentenced to death for practicing their faith.

Andrew Kim Taegon was the first native Korean to be ordained to the priesthood. Along with ministering to the Catholics in Korea, Andrew was assigned with the responsibility to arrange for missionaries to enter the country without being discovered. Unfortunately, he was caught by the authorities and arrested. Rather than renounce his faith, Andrew faced torture, and was later beheaded. Andrew was just twenty-five years old when he sacrificed his life in witness to his faith.

Persecution of Christians in Korea occurred throughout the nineteenth century. One hundred and three Christians were martyred. Among them were a few bishops and priests, but most were laypeople.

ALL ABOUT
SAINT ANDREW KIM TAEGON

- ✸ The son of Korean converts to Christianity
- ✸ Father martyred during the persecution of 1839
- ✸ Baptized at age 15
- ✸ Traveled 1,300 miles to study in the seminary in Macao, China; later returned to Korea, where he was ordained
- ✸ Canonized in 1984 with 102 other martyrs, by Pope John Paul II while on a visit to Korea

FEAST DAY: September 20, honoring Saint Andrew Kim and the Korean martyrs:

MAKE IT HAPPEN

The first three Commandments tell us of how we must live in a way that shows love for God. Love for God led Saint Andrew Kim and the other Korean martyrs to sacrifice their lives.

Describe two ways in which you can show love for God even in the face of "persecution," perhaps in the form of criticism from others or inconvenience to yourself.

_____

_____

_____

_____

_____

Catholic Social Teaching
CARE FOR GOD'S CREATION

God is the Creator of all people and all that exists in nature. He has given us the bounty of the earth and its resources and has entrusted us with its care. We are called to respond by protecting and caring for all God's creation for generations to come.

The ways to care for God's creation are countless. Choose one that you can make a part of your everyday life and make a commitment to put it into action.

YOUR TURN

A. Complete the following sentences, using words from the box.

1 _____ is the act of showing contempt for God or sacred things through one's words or actions.

2 We are required to participate in the celebration of _____ on Sundays and other Holy Days of Obligation.

3 The denial of the existence of God is called _____ .

4 Saint Andrew Kim Taegon became a _____ , giving up his life for his faith.

5 The taking of a false oath is called _____ .

6 The _____ is our God-given understanding of the created moral order that forms the basis of personal morality and civil norms.

| natural law |
| perjury |
| atheism |
| blasphemy |
| martyr |
| Mass |

B. Respond to the following.

The first three Commandments guide our relationship with God. Name each of these Commandments.

_____

_____

_____

Choose one the first three Commandments, and tell how you can live it in your own life.

_____

_____

_____

The Ten Commandments: Love Your Neighbor

A Psalm Prayer

Side 1: The law of the LORD is perfect,
refreshing the soul….

Side 2: The precepts of the LORD are right,
rejoicing the heart….

Side 1: The statutes of the LORD are true,
all of them just.

Side 2: From willful sins keep your servant;
let them never control me….

All: Let the words of my mouth meet with your favor,
keep the thoughts of my heart before you,
LORD, my rock and my redeemer.

—Psalm 19:8–10, 14–15

Live It Out

Commandments 4 through 10 guide our interactions with other people, starting with those closest to us, our families. What is the state of your relationship with your parents and with other family members? What can you do to strengthen it?

> *"You shall love the LORD your God with all your heart, with all your soul, with all your mind, and with all your strength. . . . You shall love your neighbor as yourself."*

The Great Commandment

In the Old Testament, we read of God's covenant with the Israelites, mediated by Moses, in which he gave the people of Israel the Law for living a life freed from the slavery of sin. In the Gospels, Jesus interprets the Law as a two-fold yet single commandment of love.

SACRED SCRIPTURE

A READING FROM THE HOLY GOSPEL ACCORDING TO MARK

One of the scribes, when he came forward and heard them disputing and saw how well he had answered them, asked him, "Which is the first of all the commandments?" Jesus replied, "The first is this: 'Hear, O Israel! The LORD our God is Lord alone! You shall love the LORD your God with all your heart, with all your soul, with all your mind, and with all your strength.' The second is this: 'You shall love your neighbor as yourself.' There is no other commandment greater than these." The scribe said to him, "Well said, teacher. You are right in saying, 'He is One and there is no other than he.' And 'to love him with all your heart, with all your understanding, with all your strength, and to love your neighbor as yourself' is worth more than all burnt offerings and sacrifices." And when Jesus saw that [he] answered with understanding, he said to him, "You are not far from the kingdom of God." And no one dared to ask him any more questions.

—Mark 12:28–34

Christ Teaches Humility, Robert Scott Lauder, c. 1850 (oil on canvas, Scotland)

START LIVING

Jesus summed up the Ten Commandments in two simple rules, one concerning love for God, the other love for neighbor and self.

Explain what Jesus' teaching to love your neighbor as yourself means to you.

Jesus's teachings means treat others the way you would want to be treated.

When it comes to understanding how we must treat others, Jesus explains it simply, telling us we must love our neighbor as we love ourselves. **Describe a situation in which you can use this rule to guide your actions toward another person.**

You can help shovel snow off of anyone's driveway. You can also give them a meal or anything they are in need of.

Stop and Think

Reflect on Jesus' command "You shall love your neighbor as yourself" (Mark 12:31). What are some ways you can live its message in your everyday life?

OUR CATHOLIC TRADITION

> No one has ever seen God. Yet, if we love one another, God remains in us, and his love is brought to perfection in us.
>
> —1 John 4:12

Commandments 4–10: Love of Neighbor

The first three Commandments guide our relationship with God. The remaining seven guide us in our interactions with other people. By obeying these Commandments, we follow Jesus' instruction to love our neighbor as we love ourselves. Here is what each of these Commandments means in our lives today.

4 Honor your father and your mother.

- Treat your parents with respect, gratitude, obedience, and affection. Provide them with the assistance and care they need.
- After God, we must respect and obey our parents and others whom God has vested with authority over us for our own good. Parents have a responsibility to care for their children physically and spiritually and to encourage their vocation.

5 You shall not kill.

- Murder, taking away the life of another person, is gravely wrong.
- Because every human being is made in God's image and likeness, all human life is sacred, from the moment of conception to natural death. Abortion, the termination of the life of an unborn child, violates the Fifth Commandment. We are required to treat and care for a human embryo as we would every other human being.
- **Euthanasia**, also called "mercy killing," violates human dignity and the respect we owe the Creator.
- Suicide is a rejection of God's love and love of ourselves. We must work to preserve our own lives and the lives of others.

6 You shall not commit adultery.

- Jesus is our model of **chastity**, and we are all called to be chaste and to respect our own sexuality and the sexuality of others.
- The covenant of marriage requires faithful love and sexual fidelity between husband and wife. Adultery, divorce, or sexual relationships outside of marriage violate the Sixth Commandment.

7 You shall not steal.

- Stealing, cheating, and dishonesty in any form violate this Commandment.
- God created the earth's resources for the good of all people, and unjust use of or unfair access to these resources violates God's purpose. We must work to share the earth's resources with all people and to preserve them for future generations.

8 You shall not bear false witness against your neighbor.

- Lying or in any way deliberately deceiving another person is a violation of this Commandment.
- Committing **slander**, or creating or passing on rumors or lies about another person, violates the Eighth Commandment.

9 You shall not covet your neighbor's wife.

- Our sexuality must be marked by modesty in the way we dress, speak, and act.
- We must practice restraint and show respect for others' sexuality in our thoughts, words, and actions.

10 You shall not covet your neighbor's goods.

- We must not have an excessive desire for material possessions.
- Envy, or sadness at another's good fortune is a sin against the Tenth Commandment.

CATECHISM Q&A

Q. When is a citizen forbidden to obey civil authorities?

A. We are obliged in conscience not to obey the laws of civil authorities or others who have authority over us when they are contrary to the demands of the moral order. (See *Compendium*, Question 465; *CCC*, 2256.)

Q. When is the taking of another life not a violation of the Fifth Commandment?

A. Although murder is a grave sin against the Fifth Commandment, when we legitimately defend ourselves we are choosing life, and not choosing to kill. For those responsible for the lives of others, legitimate defense is not only a right but a duty. (See *Compendium*, Question 467; *CCC*, 2321.)

COMPENDIUM
Catechism of the Catholic Church

CATECHISM *of the* CATHOLIC CHURCH
SECOND EDITION

Calendar Connection
Gratian's *Decretum*

WHO Gratian

WHAT Gratian's *Decretum*

WHERE Bologna, Italy

WHEN 1140

WHY The first collection of the Church's laws, drawn from the writings of the Church Fathers, papal pronouncements, and decrees issued by local synods and councils, was compiled by Gratian, a Benedictine monk from Bologna, and was issued in 1140. This collection, which came to be known as Gratian's *Decretum*, was the first systematic and unified collection of laws in the history of the West.

KNOW and BELIEVE

Choose two of the Commandments you learned about in this lesson and for each describe at least one way that you can better live it.

I can honor my mother and Father by respecting them and doing what they say. I can also stop thinking about material possessions.

KNOW IT!

euthanasia
bringing about the death of a sick, handicapped, or dying person either through a direct action or by taking no action; euthanasia is murder

chastity
the virtue which regulates our sexual desires, thoughts, and actions

slander
spreading lies or rumors about another person

SAINTLY *profiles*

The path to holiness is often one of countless small acts of love for God and for others, rather than grand deeds and spectacular miracles. Saint Kateri Tekakwitha is a great example of this. She lived a simple life of prayer and devotion to God and kindness and generosity to her neighbors. And because of her humility and example, she led many others to God.

Saint Kateri Tekakwitha 1656–1680

Kateri Tekakwitha was a member of the Iroquois Nation of Native Americans, and lived in what is now New York State. "Tekakwitha" was her Native American name.

When European settlers came to North America, they brought with them deadly diseases, such as small pox. Countless Native Americans died from these diseases, among them Tekakwitha's parents and brother. Tekakwitha herself contracted small pox, but she recovered. However, the disease left her face badly scarred. The orphaned and frail Tekakwitha was adopted by an aunt and uncle, who cared for her and nurtured her back to health.

When Tekakwitha was twelve years old, some white Jesuit missionaries arrived in her village. Kateri was greatly moved by their message of God's love, and eventually she asked to be baptized, taking the name Kateri, Mohawk for Catherine.

Many people in Kateri's village resented her conversion to Christianity and mistreated her because of it. Although she remained patient and forgiving, Kateri eventually decided it was best for her to leave and go live among other Christians.

In her new home, Kateri felt free to practice her faith. She developed a reputation for kindness, and cared for the sick and aged of the village. She told many stories about Jesus and his great love for all people. Kateri chose not to marry so she could fully devote her life to God, and explained that all the members of her village were her family.

At age twenty-four, Kateri became ill and soon died. After her death, her complexion became clear and radiant. Those who knew her believed this was a sign of God's blessing on Kateri and a symbol of her holiness.

ALL ABOUT
SAINT KATERI TEKAKWITHA

- Father was a Mohawk warrior; mother was a member of the Algonquin tribe
- Known as the "Lily of the Mohawks"
- Because of her example, many Native Americans were baptized into the Catholic faith
- Canonized in 2012, the first Native American declared a saint

FEAST DAY: July 14

MAKE IT HAPPEN

To love God and live according to his laws, we must also love others and treat them with kindness and dignity.

How is Kateri an example of love for God expressed through love for others, and how can you follow her example?

_____

_____

_____

_____

_____

KNOW IT!

Water

Water is essential for life, and it cleanses and renews creation. Unchecked it can also lead to destruction and death. In Baptism, water is a sign of new life and a new birth in which we are cleansed from sin and buried with Christ so as to rise to new life with him.

YOUR TURN

A. Match each Commandment in Column A with its number in Column B by writing the letter of the correct answer in the space provided.

A

a. You shall not steal.

b. You shall not commit adultery.

c. You shall not covet your neighbor's wife.

d. Honor your father and your mother.

e. You shall not covet your neighbor's goods.

f. You shall not kill.

g. You shall not bear false witness against your neighbor.

B

1. _D_ Fourth Commandment

2. _F_ Fifth Commandment

3. _B_ Sixth Commandment

4. _A_ Seventh Commandment

5. _G_ Eighth Commandment

6. _C_ Ninth Commandment

7. _E_ Tenth Commandment

B. Respond to the following.

In instructing us about how we are to treat other people, Jesus said we must love our neighbor as we love ourselves. How do Commandments 4 through 10 express Jesus' command?

_____

_____

_____

Commandments 4 through 10 guide our relationships with other people. Choose two of these Commandments, and tell how you can apply them to your own life.

_____

_____

_____

Living the Beatitudes

A Prayer of Praise

Praise the LORD, my soul;
    I shall praise the LORD all my life,
    sing praise to my God while I live.
Happy those whose …
    hope is in the LORD, their God, …
Who keeps faith forever,
    secures justice for the oppressed,
    gives food to the hungry.
The LORD sets prisoners free;
    the LORD gives sight to the blind.
The LORD raises up those who are bowed down;
    …loves the righteous,
    …but thwarts the way of the wicked.
The LORD shall reign forever.

—Psalm 146:2, 5–10

Live It Out
Taking care of others and serving those in need is a way to express God's love to others. How well do you share God's love?

> ## *"Rejoice and be glad, for your reward will be great in heaven."*

The Beatitudes

When Jesus began his public ministry, he went around all of Galilee, teaching all who would hear. Great crowds followed him. To a crowd that had gathered to hear him, Jesus taught the Beatitudes, in which he described the qualities those who are part of the Kingdom of God must have, and ways in which they will be blessed. The Beatitudes are part of what is known as the Sermon on the Mount.

SACRED SCRIPTURE

A reading from the holy Gospel according to Matthew

When Jesus saw the crowds, he went up the mountain, and after he had sat down, his disciples came to him. He began to teach them, saying:

"Blessed are the poor in spirit,
for theirs is the kingdom of heaven.
Blessed are they who mourn,
for they will be comforted.
Blessed are the meek,
for they will inherit the land.
Blessed are they who hunger and thirst for righteousness,
for they will be satisfied.
Blessed are the merciful,
for they will be shown mercy.
Blessed are the clean of heart,
for they will see God.
Blessed are the peacemakers,
for they will be called children of God.
Blessed are they who are persecuted for the sake of righteousness,
for theirs is the kingdom of heaven.
Blessed are you when they insult you and persecute you and utter every kind of evil against you falsely because of me. Rejoice and be glad, for your reward will be great in heaven."

—Matthew 5:1–12

START LIVING

In the Beatitudes, Jesus extols those who are merciful, assuring them of God's mercy.

Describe acts of mercy you show or can show in your everyday life that would be pleasing to Jesus.

_____

_____

_____

_____

_____

_____

The qualities Jesus praises in the Beatitudes are often very different from what society values. **For each of the following socially desirable qualities, provide an alternative from the Beatitudes, and tell why it is a better alternative.**

Socially Valued	The Alternative
material wealth	_____
	_____
popularity	_____
	_____
power and influence	_____
	_____

During the Mass
The Scripture passage of the Sermon on the Mount, in which Jesus teaches us the Beatitudes, is read on the Fourth Sunday of Ordinary Time during Year A. See pages 218–219.

OUR CATHOLIC TRADITION

Living the Beatitudes

All people have a desire for happiness. We search for it in many ways and seek it through many sources. For example, some people try to find happiness by buying the latest fashions. Others may believe happiness comes from social acceptance and may seek it by trying to be popular at school or among their peers. But Jesus tells us that our true happiness comes from God.

In the **Beatitudes**, Jesus helps us understand how we can achieve true happiness by living as Beatitude, or blessed, people. To live as Beatitude people, it is essential to remember that we and all people, are, from the moment of conception, created in God's image and likeness.

We, as individuals and as a society, must strive to respect the dignity of all people. As individuals, we can do this through acts of charity, by showing kindness to those in need, and by teaching others of God's love through our words and deeds. We can care for others, physically and spiritually, by performing the **Works of Mercy**. Through these loving acts, we show respect for other people's dignity and live as Jesus wants us to. The Works of Mercy are divided into two categories:

- The Corporal Works of Mercy are concerned with the physical needs of others. They include feeding the hungry and visiting the sick.
- The Spiritual Works of Mercy address the needs of the heart, mind, and soul, and include praying for others, comforting the suffering, and forgiving those who have wronged us.

In addition to our personal responsibilities, as a society we are obligated to abide by an order of creation established by God, committed to the common good. It is the duty of governments to work for and protect the common good. Responding to the needs of others is a central part of our calling as Christians. **Catholic Social Teaching** calls all members of the Church to work for justice and peace in society. It states that the purpose of every social organization must be the good of the human person. According to the principles of Catholic Social Teaching:

- Respect for all people is based on their human dignity and on the rights given each person by God.
- Political authority must be exercised within the bounds of the moral order.
- Social conditions must be created that allow people to reach their fulfillment.
- We must work to create and support institutions that improve the conditions of human life.

When we follow Jesus' teachings and live the Beatitudes, we as individuals can find happiness, and society as a whole will be made better. **(See pages 206–207 for more on the Beatitudes and the Works of Mercy.)**

CATECHISM Q&A

Q. What is the root of human dignity?

A. Our human dignity is rooted in our creation in God's image and likeness. God has endowed us with an immortal soul, intelligence, and free will, and from the moment of our conception we are called to eternal happiness with God. (See *Compendium*, Question 358; *CCC*, 1711.)

Q. What is the common good?

A. The common good is the whole of conditions of social life that allow people as groups and as individuals to reach their proper fulfillment. It is the duty of the state to promote and defend the common good. (See *Compendium*, Question 407; *CCC*, 1924.)

CATHOLIC CUSTOMS OPERATION RICE BOWL

Each Lent, many U.S. parishes participate in Catholic Relief Services' "Operation Rice Bowl." This program calls us to pray with our families and faith communities, to fast in solidarity with those who hunger, to learn more about the challenges of poverty overseas, and to give sacrificial contributions to those in need. Seventy-five percent of money raised through Operation Rice Bowl supports CRS' development projects overseas and Lenten education efforts in the U.S., and 25 percent of funds supports hunger and poverty alleviation efforts in dioceses in the U.S. To learn more or sign up to participate, visit orb.crs.org.

KNOW and BELIEVE

In what ways do you practice personal acts of charity? In what ways do you contribute to the common good?

_____

_____

_____

_____

_____

KNOW IT!

Beatitudes
Jesus' teachings about how to live and find real happiness in God's kingdom

Works of Mercy
loving deeds by which we care for the physical and spiritual needs of other people

Catholic Social Teaching
the teaching of the Church that calls us to work for justice and peace in society

SAINTLY *profiles*

ALL ABOUT
BLESSED MOTHER TERESA

✸ Worked among the "untouchables" of Indian society for nearly fifty years

✸ Received numerous awards from the Indian government, including the Jawaharlal Nehru Award for International Understanding and the Bharat Ratna, the country's highest civilian award

✸ Awarded the Nobel Peace Prize in 1979 for her tireless work serving the poor

✸ The Missionaries of Charity today number in the thousands

✸ Beatified by Pope John Paul II in 2003

Striving to live according to Jesus' teachings about how Christians must live, serving and caring for others, is not always easy. But we can learn from the example of those who fully accepted Jesus' call to serve others.

Blessed Mother Teresa 1910–1997

Mother Teresa was born Agnes Bojaxhiu, in Yugoslavia. As a young girl, she read about the works of Catholic missionaries in all parts of the world, and felt a great desire to serve as they did. She took her first step toward this goal by joining the Sisters of Our Lady of Loreto in 1928, at age eighteen. A few years later, she made her final profession as a Loreto sister, taking the name Teresa. Her first assignment as a Loreto sister was in India, where she worked as a teacher. She taught for a number of years in a school for girls from well-off families, but felt called by Christ to serve him among the poor in Indian society.

Following Christ's call, and with the archbishop's permission, Teresa left the Loreto convent and traveled to Calcutta, to live and work among the poor in the slums of the city. Encouraged by the archbishop, she soon started her own religious order, the Missionaries of Charity.

Mother Teresa and the other women who joined her missionary order founded homes where they could bring the people that lay dying on the city streets, so that they may die in dignity, treated with love and compassion. The sisters also founded orphanages where the unwanted children of Calcutta could be cared for, educated, and loved. They cared for those afflicted with leprosy, AIDS, or any other illness, as well as the abandoned and unloved.

Following the example and teachings of Jesus, Mother Teresa served the humblest and weakest members of society, those deemed of little value. Along with the physical care she provided them, she taught them of God's love and mercy.

MAKE IT HAPPEN

Choose one Beatitude and one Work of Mercy and tell how Mother Teresa lived each. Then tell how her example might guide your own actions.

Beatitude: _____

Mother Teresa's Example	What I Can Do

Work of Mercy: _____

Mother Teresa's Example	What I Can Do

Catholic Social Teaching
OPTION FOR THE POOR AND VULNERABLE

In the Beatitudes, Jesus said, "Blessed are the merciful, for they will be shown mercy" (Matthew 5:7). One way we are called to show mercy is by caring for members of our community and society who are in need—physically, economically, or emotionally.

To whom can you reach out to show kindness and mercy? How? Take steps to put your ideas into action.

LET US PRAY

Prayer of Saint Francis

Lord, make me an instrument of your peace.
Where there is hatred, let me sow love; where there is injury, pardon;
where there is doubt, faith; where there is despair, hope;
where there is darkness, light; and where there is sadness, joy.
O divine Master, grant that I may not so much seek to be consoled as to console,
to be understood as to understand, to be loved as to love;
for it is in giving that we receive, it is in pardoning that we are pardoned,
and it is in dying that we are born to eternal life.

YOUR TURN

A. Circle the letter of the correct answer.

1 The _____ are loving deeds by which we care for the physical and spiritual needs of other people.

(a) Works of Mercy   **c** Beatitudes

b Catholic Social Teaching   **d** common good

2 The _____ address the needs of the heart, mind, and soul, and include praying for others and forgiving those who have wronged us.

a Corporal Works of Mercy

b first four Beatitudes

(c) Spiritual Works of Mercy

d Catholic Social Teaching

3 The teachings of the Church that call us to work for justice and peace in society are _____ .

a the Corporal Works of Mercy

b the Sermon on the Mount

c the Beatitudes

(d) Catholic Social Teaching

4 To live as Beatitude people, we must remember that the dignity of all people is rooted in _____ .

a the common good

b the option for the poor and vulnerable

c our creation as members of society

(d) our creation in God's image and likeness

5 The _____ Works of Mercy are concerned with the physical needs of others.

~~**a** Spiritual~~   **(c)** Corporal

b Capital   **d** Common

6 Jesus' teachings about how to live and find real happiness in God's kingdom are called _____ .

(a) the Works of Mercy

(b) the Beatitudes

c Catholic Social Teaching

b the Commandments

B. Respond to the following.

Describe one way that Blessed Mother Teresa of Calcutta practiced the Corporal Works of Mercy, and one way she practiced the Spiritual Works of Mercy.

_____

_____

_____

What are some ways you could put the Works of Mercy into practice in your own life?

_____

_____

_____

Being Catholic
CHRISTIAN CHARITY IN ACTION

LIVING THE CALL TO SERVE

As Christians, we are all called to love and serve others. In the Sermon on the Mount, in which Jesus taught the Beatitudes, he also gave us the Golden Rule: "Do to others what you would have them do to you" (Matthew 7:12). This simple rule provides a perfect guide for us in how we are to treat others, especially those most in need of our kindness and mercy.

One way to serve others is through parish ministries, such as being a catechist, altar server, or choir member. For young people, the first call to serve as members of the parish community frequently comes with Confirmation preparation, when they are required to participate in a service project, such as visiting elderly residents of a nursing home or collecting canned goods for a food pantry. It's easy to look at this service project as a chore and to just count hours until the required number are met. However, by doing this, we lose an opportunity to grow spiritually by giving selflessly. Even when performing acts of charity is a requirement, we can do them out of love for others and for God and can open ourselves to the spiritual enrichment the experience provides.

What are some ways you have served others? Did you do these things because you were required to or by choice? How do you feel when you perform acts of Christian service?

> "Confirmation gives us special strength to witness to and glorify God with our whole lives. It makes us intimately aware of our belonging to the Church, the Body of Christ, of which we are all living members, in solidarity with one another."
>
> —Pope Benedict XVI, message to the Young People of the World during World Youth Day, July 20, 2008

LIVING OUT OUR BAPTISMAL CALL

At our baptism, the priest or deacon anointed us with the oil of Sacred Chrism, saying, "Remain forever a member of Christ who is Priest, Prophet, and King" *(Rite of Baptism).* We are called to live this baptismal call to follow Christ in being priest, prophet, and king.

Priest	All baptized people share in the priesthood of Christ, and make up the priesthood of the faithful.	Whenever we sacrifice our time for someone, such as by praying for a friend or relative, we are being priest for that person.
Prophet	A prophet is someone who proclaims God's truth or stands up for the Catholic faith.	This is often the most difficult of the three roles to identify with, because it often requires us to stand apart from others.
King	Jesus was a servant King because he selflessly put the needs of others before himself.	Dying on the cross for us is the greatest example of this selfless love. "No one has greater love than this, to lay down ones life for one's friend" (John 15:13).

Jesus is not asking us to die on a cross, but he does ask us to serve and love others as he loves us. Whenever we offer service to the community and lead by example, we are fulfilling our baptismal role as King.

Share one way you have been priest, prophet, or king.

ANSWERING THE CALL TO SERVE

You can live out your call to be priest, prophet, and king through service to the Church. By offering ourselves to God in all we do and in our service to others, we are united to the sacrifice of Christ in the Mass. Each of us is called to play particular roles in service to the Church. For example, your talents may lead you to serve the Church and your parish community by singing in the church choir or by reading at Mass. Or you may enjoy volunteering at your parish's vacation Bible school. After participating in an event or project, people often find that instead of it being a chore, it was actually an enjoyable experience that they were able to learn and grow from. Participating in Christian service is a great way to discover what God wants you to do in service to the Church.

How can you increase your service to others and to the Church by sharing your special gifts to help others through one or more parish ministries?

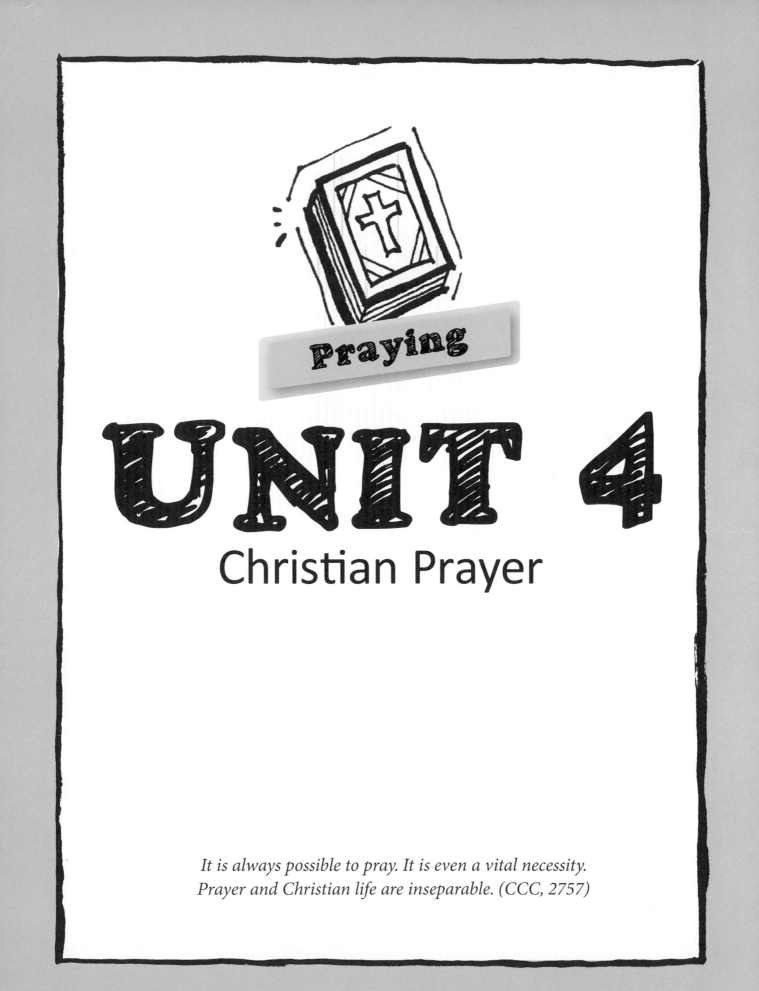

Praying

UNIT 4
Christian Prayer

It is always possible to pray. It is even a vital necessity. Prayer and Christian life are inseparable. (CCC, 2757)

The Lord's Prayer

Our Father, who art in heaven,

hallowed be thy name.

Thy kingdom come;

Thy will be done

on earth, as it is in heaven.

Give us this day our daily bread,

and forgive us our trespasses,

as we forgive those

who trespass against us,

and lead us not into temptation,

but deliver us from evil.

Amen.

Prayer in the Christian Life

A Prayer of Trust

All: I love the LORD, who listened
to my voice in supplication,
Who turned an ear to me
on the day I called.

Side 1: Gracious is the LORD and just;
yes, our God is merciful.
The LORD protects the simple;
I was helpless, but God saved me.

All: I love the LORD, who listened
to my voice in supplication,
Who turned an ear to me
on the day I called.

Side 2: My soul has been freed from death,
my eyes from tears, my feet
from stumbling.
I shall walk before the LORD
in the land of the living.

All: I love the LORD, who listened
to my voice in supplication,
Who turned an ear to me
on the day I called.

—Psalm 116:1–2, 5–6, 8–9

Live It Out
Is prayer a daily part of your life? How does prayer help you grow in your relationship with God?

"But when the Son of Man comes, will he find faith on earth?"

The Parable of the Persistent Widow

Jesus taught his disciples the importance of praying, and of doing so without growing weary or impatient. In the **Parable** of the Persistent Widow, he compares how we must approach God in prayer to the way the widow approached the harsh judge: She continued to go to him in hope of a favorable decision. In the same way, we must continue to turn to God, who is loving and benevolent, and who answers our prayers in ways we sometimes do not recognize or understand.

SACRED SCRIPTURE

A reading from the holy Gospel according to Luke

Then [Jesus] told them a parable about the necessity for them to pray always without becoming weary. He said, "There was a judge in a certain town who neither feared God nor

respected any human being. And a widow in that town used to come to him and say, 'Render a just decision for me against my adversary.' For a long time the judge was unwilling, but eventually he thought, 'While it is true that I neither fear God nor respect any human being, because this widow keeps bothering me I shall deliver a just verdict for her lest she finally come and strike me.'" The Lord said, "Pay attention to what the dishonest judge says. Will not God then secure the rights of his chosen ones who call out to him day and night? Will he be slow to answer them? I tell you, he will see to it that justice is done for them speedily. But when the Son of Man comes, will he find faith on earth?"

—Luke 18:1–8

START LIVING

The judge in Jesus' parable about how we must pray has no regard for God's laws or people's needs. He was indifferent to the widow's plight, but in the end gave her what she wanted because she persisted, and he just wanted her to leave him alone. When we pray to God, our loving Father, his response is immensely different than that of the judge.

What does the Parable of the Persistent Widow tell you about how to approach God in prayer?

How can seeing God as a loving Father help you accept the way he responds to your prayers?

Stop and Think

Reread Jesus' words at the end of the Parable of the Persistent Widow. Reflect on their meaning, and in your own words explain Jesus' message about how God hears and answers our prayers.

OUR CATHOLIC TRADITION

God Calls Us to Pray

What is your idea of prayer? Do you imagine kneeling in church at Mass, or perhaps saying a few words to God in the privacy of your room before you go to sleep? Is prayer a conversation with God in which you ask him to grant you certain requests or thank him for specific blessings? While these are ways to pray and reasons for doing so, this should be just the beginning of the place of prayer in the life of a Christian.

Thinking of prayer as a conversation with God is a good start. But like any good conversation, prayer requires talking as well as listening. Prayer is defined as the raising of one's mind and heart to God or the requesting of good things from God. According to the first part of this definition, prayer also requires a silent focus on God, allowing an opportunity for him to speak to our hearts and for us to grow in our understanding of who he is. God calls us to meet him and welcome him in our hearts in this way. Of course, when we pray we can also ask God to grant our needs or those of others, but we must always be open to accepting God's will in the way he responds.

In addition to making requests from God when we pray, there are many other reasons to pray. Basic forms of Christian prayer, modeled on the Book of Psalms, include prayers of blessing, petition, intercession, thanksgiving, and praise. **(See page 195 for more on the five basic forms of prayer.)**

In the words of Saint Paul, we must "pray without ceasing" (1 Thessalonians 5:17). This means that we must form a habit of praying daily and in a deliberate manner. When we pray, we primarily address our prayers to God the Father. A prayerful relationship with God can be developed through various forms of prayer, and does not always require us to address God with words. Of course, this way of praying, called vocal prayer, is probably the most familiar to most of us. Vocal prayer can include the recitation of traditional prayers, such as the Lord's Prayer, as well as talking to God in our own words to tell him of our needs, hopes, and our love for him. We can also pray through **meditation**. Meditation is a form of silent prayer that engages our minds, imagination, and emotions in reflecting on and coming to a deeper understanding of God's message to us, as revealed through Scripture or through the Church. One common way to engage in meditative prayer is through *lectio divina* (lex-ee-oh di-vee-na), or holy reading. This method of prayer involves reading a Scripture passage and meditating on its meaning. Similar to meditation is **contemplation**; however, this form of prayer involves simply being fully in the presence of God—an awareness arrived at through our feelings of love for God.

Through the Holy Spirit, we can develop a deeper relationship with God through prayer.

CATECHISM Q&A

Q. Where can we first learn to pray?

A. Our family is the first place we can learn to pray. Daily family prayer is especially important because it is the first witness to a life of prayer in the Church. (See *Compendium*, Question 565; CCC, 2694.)

Q. What are the difficulties in prayer?

A. Distraction and dryness are common challenges to prayer. The easiest way to overcome them is by turning our attention back to God, rather than turning away from him, and persisting in prayer. (See *Compendium*, Question 574; CCC, 2729, 2731.)

COMPENDIUM
Catechism of the Catholic Church

CATECHISM of the CATHOLIC CHURCH
SECOND EDITION

KNOW and BELIEVE

What is your favorite time of day to pray? Reflect on ways you can address God in prayer throughout the day.

_____

_____

_____

_____

_____

_____

_____

Calendar Connection
Edict of Milan

WHO Emperors Constantine I and Licinius

WHAT *Edict of Milan*

WHERE Roman Empire

WHEN A.D. 313

WHY To stop the frequent persecution of the early Christians, the emperors Constantine I and Licinius issued the *Edict of Milan* in the year 313. In it, they granted to Christians the right to worship as they wished, and returned to the Church properties and other possessions that had been confiscated from it.

KNOW IT!

meditation
a form of silent prayer in which we engage our thoughts, imagination, and emotions to understand a particular truth, Scripture message, or other spiritual matter

contemplation
a form of silent prayer in which we are deeply focused on the presence of God

SAINTLY *profiles*

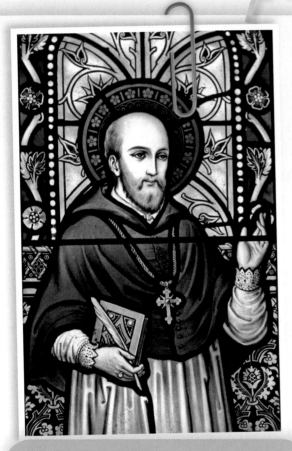

ALL ABOUT
SAINT FRANCIS DE SALES

❋ Taught that the key to love of God was prayer: "By turning your eyes on God in meditation, your whole soul will be filled with God."

❋ Influential writings include *Introduction to the Devout Life* and *Treatise on the Love of God* as well as many pamphlets and letters

❋ Named a Doctor of the Church by Pope Pius IX in 1877

FEAST DAY: January 24
PATRONAGE: journalists and writers

Learning to form a deep prayer relationship with God is not always easy. Many people in our lives as well as in the Church can teach us how to pray more deeply, more meaningfully, and more frequently. Saint Francis de Sales is one such person. His personal example and his writings provide us with guidance on the importance of prayer in our lives.

Saint Francis de Sales 1567–1622

Francis de Sales was born in France. He was educated by the Jesuits at the finest schools in Savoy. As a young man, he studied law and theology at the University of Padua, and earned a doctorate in both disciplines. It was during this period of his life that Francis felt called by God to dedicate his life to the service of the Church.

Although his father had secured for him a number of prestigious positions, including one as a senator in Savoy, Francis turned down these opportunities, and instead revealed his desire to become a priest. As a priest, and later as bishop, Francis had a reputation as a captivating preacher. He was also known for his generosity to the poor and his good-natured manner.

Francis' first assignment after ordination was as administrator of the Diocese of Geneva, a Protestant stronghold with strong anti-Catholic sentiment. Through his homilies and writings, Father Francis was a powerful defender of Catholic doctrine against Protestant attacks, and was successful in winning many back to the Catholic faith. He also wrote extensively on the importance of prayer and holiness in the lives of all people.

Francis de Sales' writings include *Introduction to the Devout Life*. In this book, he wrote to Christians in all walks of life of the need for prayer and devotion to God, and stressed the importance of the Sacraments as a means for obtaining grace and growing in holiness. This book on prayer was immensely popular when it was first published and is still recognized as a classic Christian text.

MAKE IT HAPPEN

Saint Francis de Sales stressed the importance of prayer for all people, in all circumstances.

How often and how well do you pray—that is, how focused are you on God when you pray? Name times of the day when you can pray, and set a goal for yourself to do so. Then describe how you can prepare yourself for prayer so that you are more attuned to God's presence.

Times of day I can pray:

_____

_____

_____

Ways to pray better:

_____

_____

_____

KNOW IT!

Lilies

Lilies symbolize the Resurrection of Jesus Christ, because just as these beautiful springtime flowers bloom from a seemingly lifeless bulb, so Jesus rises from the dead.

LET US PRAY

A Meditation Prayer

Jesus Calms the Storm at Sea

[Jesus] got into a boat and his disciples followed him. Suddenly, a violent storm came up on the sea, so that the boat was being swamped by waves; but he was asleep. They came and woke him, saying, "Lord, save us! We are perishing!" He said to them, "Why are you terrified, O you of little faith?" Then he got up, rebuked the winds and the sea, and there was great calm. The men were amazed and said, "What sort of man is this, whom even the winds and the sea obey?"

—Matthew 8:23–27

YOUR TURN

A. Complete the following sentences.

1 A _____ is a story that illustrates a moral truth or a religious principle.

2 Like any good conversation, _____ requires talking as well as listening to God.

3 In his *Introduction to the Devout Life*, Francis de Sales wrote of the need for prayer and devotion to God, and stressed the importance of the _____ as a means for obtaining grace and growing in holiness.

4 _____ is a form of silent prayer in which we are deeply focused on the presence of God.

5 _____ is a form of silent prayer in which we engage our thoughts, imagination, and emotions to understand a particular truth, Scripture message, or other spiritual matter.

6 *Lectio divina*, a method of prayer whose name means " _____ ," involves reading a Scripture passage and meditating on its meaning.

B. Respond to the following.

Briefly describe each of the following basic forms of Christian prayer.

prayer of blessing: _____

prayer of petition: _____

prayer of intercession: _____

prayer of thanksgiving: _____

prayer of praise: _____

Write a prayer in your own words, using one of the forms of Christian prayer.

_____

_____

_____

_____

The Lord's Prayer

Praying with Psalm 23

The LORD is my shepherd;
    there is nothing I lack.
In green pastures you let me graze;
    to safe waters you lead me;
    you restore my strength.
You guide me along the right path
    for the sake of your name.
Even when I walk through a dark valley,
    I fear no harm for you are at my side;
    your rod and staff give me courage.
You set a table before me
    as my enemies watch;
You anoint my head with oil;
    my cup overflows.
Only goodness and love will pursue me
    all the days of my life;
I will dwell in the house of the LORD
    for years to come.

—Psalm 23:1–6

Live It Out
Jesus taught us to call God our Father, and to trust in his loving goodness. How can the words of Psalm 23 help you visualize God as a loving Father?

BIBLE BOOST

> *This is how you are to pray: Our Father, in heaven, hallowed be your name.*

The Lord's Prayer

In Matthew's Gospel, in his preaching at the Sermon on the Mount, Jesus taught his disciples the Lord's Prayer. This prayer, also called the Our Father, contains seven petitions that together form a summary of all that we need to live a Christian life.

SACRED SCRIPTURE

A READING FROM THE HOLY GOSPEL ACCORDING TO MATTHEW

The Lord's Prayer, Pater Noster, c. 1890 (watercolor and gouache on paperboard, France)

This is how you are to pray:
Our Father, in heaven,
 hallowed be your name,
 your kingdom come,
 your will be done,
 on earth as in heaven.
Give us today our daily bread;
and forgive us our debts,
 as we forgive our debtors;
and do not subject us to the final test,
 but deliver us from the evil one.
    —Matthew 6:9–13

START LIVING

The Lord's Prayer begins by addressing God with the words "Our Father, in heaven."

Reflect on these words, then describe some thoughts and feelings they evoke in you. That is, what does it mean to you to be able to pray to God as Father?

In the Lord's Prayer we pray, "Forgive us our debts as we forgive our debtors," or, more commonly, "Forgive us our trespasses as we forgive those who trespass against us." **Describe the meaning of this verse as it relates to how you treat those who wrong you and how you would like God to treat you when you do wrong.**

During the Mass
The Gospel reading from Matthew in which Jesus teaches his disciples the Lord's Prayer is read during the Ritual Mass for the Presentation of the Lord's Prayer in the Rite of Christian Initiation of Adults.

OUR CATHOLIC TRADITION

Jesus Teaches Us to Pray

When Jesus taught his disciples about prayer during the Sermon on the Mount, he taught that in prayer we are to address God as Father. Jesus himself in addressing God called on him with the name *Abba*, which meant "daddy" to the Jewish people. In the Lord's Prayer, so called because Jesus is the author of the prayer, we begin by calling on God as Father.

Saint Thomas Aquinas called the Lord's Prayer the most perfect of prayers, and Saint Augustine described it as containing all that is in the Scriptures. The Lord's Prayer is truly the summary of the whole Gospel, because it expresses all that the Scriptures reveal about God and about his plan of salvation. The seven petitions of the Lord's Prayer contain all that we need to live as Christians. By looking at each of the seven petitions, we can more fully understand all that the Lord's Prayer encompasses.

Petitions 1–3

The first three petitions of the Lord's Prayer are focused on God and give him the glory and honor that he is due.

Hallowed be thy name. *Hallowed* means to be made holy. We do not make God's name holy; God is the source of his own holiness.

Thy kingdom come. This petition refers primarily to the final coming of the reign of God, at the Second Coming of Christ. But the Church is also a sign of the Kingdom of God here on earth, and when we pray "thy kingdom come" we are praying for the Church's mission of salvation for all people and committing ourselves to its work.

Thy will be done on earth as it is in heaven. We ask God to unite our will to that of Jesus so that the plan of salvation in the world may be fulfilled. We pray that God will help us obey his will, following the example Jesus gave us.

Petitions 4–7

These petitions have to do with human needs—the needs of the body and soul—for ourselves and for the whole human family.

Give us this day our daily bread. We ask God to provide us with all our earthly needs and those of the whole human family. We acknowledge that we are dependent on God, and recognize his goodness in caring for us.

Forgive us our trespasses as we forgive those who trespass against us. We ask God to forgive us when we sin, and ask him to help us be more forgiving of others who hurt us.

And lead us not into temptation. Here we ask God to help us avoid sin. We entrust ourselves to the Holy Spirit so that we may be aware of temptations and have the grace to resist sin.

But deliver us from evil. This is a prayer in union with the whole Church that God's goodness will prevail against the evil that exists in the world.

CATECHISM Q&A

Q. What spirit of communion does praying the Lord's Prayer foster?

A. The Lord's Prayer brings us into communion with the Father and with his Son, Jesus Christ. Praying to our Father is to pray with all people and for all people, that they may know the one true God. (See *Compendium*, Question 585; *CCC*, 2799.)

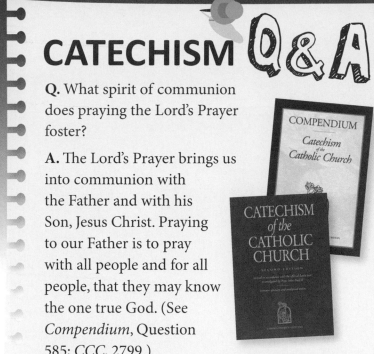

Q. Why can we address God as Father?

A. We can call God "Father" because Jesus taught us to call him "Father." Doing so should develop in us the will to act like his children, and foster in us a humble and trusting heart. (See *Compendium*, Question 583; *CCC*, 2800.)

CATHOLIC CUSTOMS
FRIDAY AS A DAY OF PENANCE

If you ask a Catholic about his or her oldest memories of Lent, most would probably respond, "No meat on Fridays!" Indeed, abstaining from meat and poultry on Fridays during Lent is a traditional penitential practice. But the fact is that the Church designates every Friday, except for solemnities, as a day of penance. Outside Lent, works of charity or devotions may be substituted for abstinence from meat. Such a discipline is meant to help us master the art of self-sacrifice and grow in love for others.

KNOW and BELIEVE

Choose one of the last four petitions from the Lord's Prayer and reflect on its meaning. How can this petition strengthen your trust in God?

_____

_____

_____

_____

_____

_____

SAINTLY *profiles*

In the Lord's Prayer, we ask God to care for all our needs, material and spiritual, and entrust our lives to his will. Sometimes we may find it challenging to accept God's will, but we can learn to trust God to lead us in a way that is best for us and that fulfills his plan for salvation.

Saint Elizabeth Ann Seton
1774–1821

Elizabeth Ann Seton was born into an affluent Episcopalian family in New York City. At age twenty, Elizabeth married William Seton, a wealthy shipping merchant. Elizabeth and William were deeply in love, and the first years of their marriage were happy and prosperous. The couple had five children.

When Elizabeth was about twenty-nine years old, her life began to change unexpectedly and dramatically. William was diagnosed with tuberculosis. In an effort to save his life, the Setons traveled to Italy, where the mild climate might aid in his recovery, but William died soon after their arrival. Elizabeth stayed on in Italy, at the home of the Filicchi family, longtime friends of her husband. The family's companionship and support comforted her during this difficult time in her life. She was deeply moved by their Catholic faith, and was inspired to learn more about their prayer and worship.

When Elizabeth returned to the United States, she continued to learn about the Catholic faith, and about a year later joined the Catholic Church. Continuing her earlier mission of service to others,

ALL ABOUT
SAINT ELIZABETH ANN SETON

* As a young mother raising five children, founded the Society for the Relief of Poor Widows with Small Children
* Family strongly disapproved of her conversion
* Canonized: September 14, 1975, the first native-born American saint

FEAST DAY: January 4
PATRONAGE: Catholic schools

and at the invitation of Bishop John Carroll of Baltimore, Elizabeth started a Catholic school in that city. Along with a few other women, she formed a religious community called the Sisters of Charity. Elizabeth Ann Seton pronounced her religious vows in March 1809, and became known as Mother Seton. The newly established religious order made provisions for Elizabeth to continue raising her children. The Sisters of Charity operated schools, hospitals, and orphanages and dedicated themselves to the care of the poor.

MAKE IT HAPPEN

In the Lord's Prayer we pray, "Thy will be done."

What were some times in Saint Elizabeth Ann Seton's life when she accepted difficulties as God's will?

_____

_____

_____

How does her example inspire you to put your trust in God?

_____

_____

_____

Catholic Social Teaching
DIGNITY OF WORK AND THE RIGHTS OF WORKERS

The Catholic Church is concerned with economic and social matters because the ultimate end of these institutions is God. The Church teaches that through labor all people participate in the work of Creation, and that all workers have the following rights and that these rights must be protected: the right to productive work, to fair wages, and to pursue economic opportunity. As Catholics we believe that our work can be a valuable way to serve God and others.

Identify one talent that you have, and make a commitment to use it in the service of God and others.

LET US PRAY

The Lord's Prayer

Our Father, who art in heaven,
hallowed be thy name.
Thy kingdom come.
Thy will be done on earth, as it is in heaven.
Give us this day our daily bread,
and forgive us our trespasses
as we forgive those who trespass against us,
and lead us not into temptation,
but deliver us from evil. Amen.

YOUR TURN

A. Circle the letter of the correct answer.

1 Jesus taught his disciples the Lord's Prayer during _____ .

a Lent

b the Agony in the Garden

c the Sermon on the Mount

d a time of Christian persecution

2 The Our Father is also called "the Lord's prayer" because _____ .

a it is the prayer Jesus prayed

b Jesus is the author of the prayer

c it is the most perfect of prayers

d it is part of the Sermon on the Mount

3 The Lord's Prayer is a summary of the _____ , because it expresses all that the Scriptures reveal about God and about his plan of salvation.

a Sermon on the Mount

b Old Testament

c writings of Saint Thomas Aquinas

d whole Gospel

4 The _____ of the Lord's Prayer are focused on God and give him the glory and honor that he is due.

a second set of petitions

b last petition

c first petition

d first three petitions

5 The _____ of the Lord's Prayer have to do with human needs for ourselves and the whole human family.

a second set of petitions

b last petition

c first petition

d first three petitions

6 "Hallowed" means _____ .

a to be empty inside

b to be in communion with the Father and with Jesus

c to unite our wills to that of Jesus

d to be made holy

B. Respond to the following.

What are some of Saint Elizabeth Ann Seton's contributions to the Church in the United States?

_____

_____

How can Saint Elizabeth's example help you to become more aware of the needs of others?

_____

_____

_____

_____

Enriching Christian Prayer: Sacramentals and Devotions

A Prayer of Thanksgiving

All: I give you thanks, O Lord.

Side 1: God indeed is my savior;
    I am confident and unafraid.
My strength and my courage is the Lord,
    and he has been my savior.

All: I give you thanks, O Lord.

Side 2: Give thanks to the Lord,
acclaim his name;
    among the nations make known his deeds,
    proclaim how exalted is his name.

All: I give you thanks, O Lord.

—Isaiah 12:1, 2, 4

Live It Out
How do you give thanks to God for his goodness? How are you an example of his goodness in the world?

BIBLE BOOST

> "But when you pray, go to your inner room, close the door, and pray to your Father in secret. And your Father who sees in secret will repay you."

Jesus Teaches About Prayer and Almsgiving

At the Sermon on the Mount, in his discourse on prayer, Jesus warned his disciples against doing good in order to be seen, and gave three specific examples of ways some might do this: **almsgiving**, praying, and fasting. Jesus said that those who do good deeds in order to be seen and praised are hypocrites, just playing a part rather than acting out of true faith.

SACRED SCRIPTURE

A READING FROM THE HOLY GOSPEL ACCORDING TO MATTHEW

[Jesus said to his disciples:] "Take care not to perform righteous deeds in order that people may see them; otherwise, you will have no recompense from your heavenly Father. When you give alms, do not blow a trumpet before you, as the hypocrites do in the synagogues and in the streets to win the praise of others. Amen, I say to you, they have received

their reward. But when you give alms, do not let your left hand know what your right is doing, so that your almsgiving may be kept secret. And your Father who sees in secret will repay you.

"When you pray, do not be like the hypocrites, who love to stand and pray in the synagogues and on street corners so that others may see them. Amen, I say to you, they have received their reward. But when you pray, go to your inner room, close the door, and pray to your Father in secret. And your Father who sees in secret will repay you.

"When you fast, do not look gloomy like the hypocrites. They neglect their appearance, so that they may appear to others to be fasting. Amen, I say to you, they have received their reward. But when you fast, anoint your head and wash your face, so that you may not appear to others to be fasting, except to your Father who is hidden. And your Father who sees what is hidden will repay you."

—Matthew 6:1–6, 16–18

START LIVING

There are times when you might feel underappreciated and want others to acknowledge your effort or good deeds. However, Jesus said, "Your Father who sees in secret will repay you" (Matthew 6:18).

KNOW iT!

almsgiving
voluntarily giving money or material goods for the aid of the poor or needy

---

How can Jesus' message affect your outlook when you do a good deed that seems to go unnoticed?

_____
_____
_____
_____

What are some ways you can live Jesus' message to pray, give alms, and fast privately?

_____
_____
_____
_____
_____
_____
_____

Stop and Think

Choose a phrase from Jesus' discourse on private prayer and reflect on ways you can apply its message to your own life.

_____
_____
_____

OUR CATHOLIC TRADITION

> "Your light must shine before others, that they may see your good deeds and glorify your heavenly Father."
>
> —Matthew 5:16

Enriching Prayer with Sacramentals and Devotions

Our prayer lives and participation in the sacraments can be enriched by a number of symbols, rituals, and devotional prayers that the church has established as part of our Catholic practices.

Sacramentals

Sacramentals are objects or actions that are usually accompanied by a special prayer. They include blessings; actions such as processions or blessing ourselves with holy water while making the Sign of the Cross or having our throat blessed (on the Feast of Saint Blaise, typically); and objects, such as holy water, candles, ashes, and medals and statues of saints.

The Church instituted sacramentals to enrich us in receiving the fruits of the sacraments, and to sanctify, or make holy, the variety of circumstances of our lives. Among the sacramentals, blessings hold an important place. A common blessing you probably know is the blessing of meals, in which we pray the Grace Before

Meals or another prayer. All blessings praise God for his gifts. Blessings usually address the Blessed Trinity through the Sign of the Cross. Sprinkling with holy water may also accompany a blessing. There are blessings for objects, such as a religious medal; blessings of people, often consecrating them for a special purpose for God; and blessings of places, such as a home or a school.

Devotions

Through the centuries, the Christian faithful have developed numerous forms of popular **devotions** to enrich their spiritual lives. While devotions are distinct from the Mass and other sacramental rites, they are part of the liturgical life of the Church. Popular devotions include the Stations of the Cross, pilgrimages to the Holy Land or to Marian shrines; participating in holy day processions; wearing Marian medals; venerating statues and sacred relics; and receiving blessed ashes on Ash Wednesday. Often, devotions have their origins in a specific culture, and may be common only to that culture. For example, the devotion to Our Lady of Guadalupe is especially important to the people of Mexico and Central America, as well as among Hispanic Americans. Among popular devotions, the Rosary holds a special place because of its relationship to the Paschal Mystery and to the faith of the Virgin Mary.

Popular forms of piety express a desire to proclaim one's faith and enrich Christian life; however, they are intended to accompany liturgical practices, and not as a substitute for them. This means that we must remember that worshiping God through participation in the Mass and the Sacraments is our most important form of prayer.

CATECHISM Q&A

Q. What are sacramentals?

A. Sacramentals are sacred signs instituted by the Church to sanctify different circumstances of life. They often include a prayer accompanied by the Sign of the Cross. (See *Compendium*, Question 351; *CCC*, 1679.)

Q. What forms of popular piety accompany the sacramental life of the Church?

A. Forms of popular piety that accompany the Church's liturgy and nourish the Christian's life include pilgrimages, processions, the Rosary, and the Stations of the Cross. (See *Compendium*, Question 353; *CCC*, 1679.)

COMPENDIUM
Catechism of the Catholic Church

CATECHISM
of the
CATHOLIC
CHURCH

ROME

Calendar Connection
Lateran Treaty

WHO Holy See and the government of Italy

WHAT Lateran Treaty

WHERE Vatican City

WHEN 1929

WHY From 754 to 1870, the papacy exercised civil authority over a number of Italian "states." As a movement to unite Italy took root, the Holy See lost control of those lands. On February 11, 1929, the Holy See and the government of Italy signed the Lateran Treaty. This agreement established the modern-day Vatican City as an independent state.

KNOW and BELIEVE

Name a devotion that you would like to learn more about and make a part of your prayer life. Tell why you chose the devotion and how it can enrich your prayer life. Make a commitment to praying this devotion often.

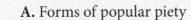

_____

_____

_____

_____

_____

KNOW IT!

sacramentals
objects or actions that signify spiritual effects that we obtain through the sacraments and that make holy the variety of circumstances of our lives

devotions
forms of prayer that, while distinct from Mass and other sacramental rites, are part of the liturgical life of the Church

Saint Francis of Assisi 1182–1226

Francis of Assisi was the son of a wealthy cloth merchant. As a young man, he lived a life of ease and pleasure. After experiencing a serious illness, however, he began to search for a greater purpose for his life. Not long after, Francis encountered a leper begging in the streets. Moved with compassion for the man, Francis embraced him and shared with him his belongings. Francis began to spend more time in the company of the poor. He soon renounced all his wealth and began to live as a mendicant, or a beggar, relying on others' charity for all his needs. He devoted his time to praying, preaching the Gospel, and serving the poor.

Francis' way of life attracted many other young men. Although it had never been Francis' plan to start a religious order, his followers formed what became the Franciscan Order of religious—a mendicant order of friars dedicated to preaching the Gospel.

In his own life and in his rule for his religious order, Saint Francis stressed the importance of poverty and simplicity. He is known for his deep prayer life, and his ability to experience God in all of nature. He is credited with bringing reform to the Church during a time when many in the Church were too focused on power and wealth.

ALL ABOUT
SAINT FRANCIS

* Known for creating the first crèche, or nativity scene, in preparation for Christmas
* Prayer for peace, now called the Prayer of Saint Francis, is attributed to him
* Founded the Franciscan Order of religious
* Canonized in 1228, just two years after his death

FEAST DAY: October 4

SAINT DOMINIC

* Founded the Dominican Order of Religious
* Known for practicing strict self-denial and long periods of fasting
* Credited with the spread of the Rosary
* Canonized in 1284

FEAST DAY: August 8

Saint Dominic 1170–1221

Saint Dominic was born at Caleruega, in northern Spain. As a young man he studied at the University of Palencia. He is the founder of the Order of Friars Preacher, also known as the Dominicans. Dominic determined that friars in his order were also to be well educated, so as to better explain and defend the truths of the Catholic faith. He encouraged the friars to spend time in study.

Dominicans adopted a spirit of poverty, so that their discipline and complete reliance on God might make them better preachers. With the Franciscans, the Dominicans formed the "Mendicants," religious orders that rely on charity for their support.

Among his contributions to the Church, Saint Dominic is credited with the spread of the Rosary. According to legend, the Blessed Virgin Mary appeared to him as he prayed in the forest and presented him with the Rosary to help him fight heresies.

MAKE IT HAPPEN

Saint Francis and Saint Dominic made significant contributions to the Church that still influence the Church today.

Choose one of these two saints, and reflect on what you have learned about him. Then describe one way that you can apply his example to your own life.

_____

_____

_____

_____

_____

KNOW IT!

INRI
These letters are the abbreviation of the Latin phrase that Pilate ordered inscribed above Jesus as he hung on the cross: *"Iesus Nazarenus Rex Iudaeorum"* ("Jesus of Nazareth, King of the Jews").

LET US PRAY

A Scripture Reflection

Leader: *During the Sermon on the Mount, Jesus spoke about how to store treasure for eternal life, rather than worry about material possessions. He said,*

Reader: *"Do not store up for yourselves treasures on earth, where moth and decay destroy, and thieves break in and steal. But store up treasures in heaven, where neither moth nor decay destroy, nor thieves break in and steal. For where your treasure is, there also will your heart be."*

—Matthew 6:19–21

YOUR TURN

A. Match Column A with Column B by writing the letter of the correct answer in the space provided.

A		B	
a. almsgiving		**1.** _____	a sacramental typically administered on the feast of Saint Blaise
b. sacramental		**2.** _____	the practice of voluntarily giving money or material goods for the aid of the poor or needy
c. devotion		**3.** _____	a form of prayer that complements the liturgical prayer of the Church
d. the Rosary		**4.** _____	an object or action that signifies spiritual effects that we obtain through the sacraments and that makes holy the variety of circumstances of our lives
e. blessing of throats		**5.** _____	a manger or Nativity scene for Christmas, made popular by Saint Francis of Assisi
f. crèche		**6.** _____	a popular and common devotion to the Blessed Mother, made popular by Saint Dominic

B. Respond to the following.

In what ways did Saint Francis and Saint Dominic show a complete reliance on and devotion to God in the religious orders they founded?

_____

_____

_____

What can you learn from the example of Saints Dominic and Francis about what is truly important in your life?

_____

_____

_____

_____

Being Catholic
OUR VOCATION

WHAT AM I SUPPOSED TO DO WITH MY LIFE?

"What do you want to be when you grow up?" This question has been asked of us since we were young children. Many people have a tough time answering it. Even adults sometimes feel like they are still looking for an answer. Discovering and using our gifts and talents can help shape who we are and what we feel called to do. Still, the age-old question should be rephrased, asking instead, "What do you think God wants you to do with your life?" If we truly live our lives for God, making choices for our future becomes a process of discerning and responding to God's will, rather than simply choosing what we want.

What do you feel God is calling you to do with your life?

> "By allowing themselves to be guided by the Spirit, each baptized person can bring his or her own contribution to the building up of the Church because of the charisms given by the Spirit, for 'to each is given the manifestation of the Spirit for the common good.' "
>
> —Pope Benedict XVI, message to the Young People of the World on World Youth Day, July 20, 2008

THE GIFTS OF THE HOLY SPIRIT

At our Confirmation, the bishop prays a special prayer during the Laying on of Hands. This prayer invokes the Holy Spirit to come upon and strengthen those about to receive the Sacrament.

All-powerful God, Father of our Lord Jesus Christ,
by water and the Holy Spirit
you freed yours sons and daughters from sin
and gave them new life.
Send your Holy Spirit upon them
to be their Helper and Guide.
Give them the spirit of wisdom and understanding,
the spirit of right judgment and courage,
the spirit of knowledge and reverence.
Fill them with the spirit of wonder and awe
in your presence.
We ask this through Christ our Lord. Amen.
—Rite of Confirmation

NO RETURNS OR EXCHANGES

What do you do when you receive a gift at Christmas or on your birthday? Do you unwrap it right away or leave it unopened? Do you choose not to use it or return it? What can you do with the Seven Gifts of the Holy Spirit? Each of these gifts can help you at different times and in different aspects of your life. Together, the Gifts of the Holy Spirit can guide you in living your life as God wants you to live it.

Wisdom—the gift of knowing what God's will is for us

Understanding—the gift of knowing how God wants us to live by loving and serving others

Counsel (Right Judgment)—the gift of knowing what is right and what is wrong and the strength to make good choices

Fortitude (Courage)—the gift of having the strength to face and overcome difficult choices and decisions

Knowledge—the gift of discovering more about God and all he has revealed through Jesus Christ.

Piety (Reverence)—the gift of respecting God and all of Creation

Fear of the Lord (Wonder and Awe)—the gift of recognizing how infinitely amazing God truly is

Choose one gift of the Spirit that you especially want to grow in, and explain how this gift can help you.

LIVING BEYOND CONFIRMATION

Often, those preparing for Confirmation think that once they receive the sacrament, they are "finished" with religion. But Confirmation is not "Catholic graduation" or the end of religious discovery. It is actually a beginning. Therefore, in Confirmation we become closer to Christ and are asked to become active members of the Church. We do this by living out our vocation, our call to live a life of holiness through the priesthood or **religious life**, married life, or single life, as well as through a particular profession or service. Through Confirmation, we receive the fullness of God's Spirit and use the Gifts of the Holy Spirit to give us the grace to live out our faith in today's world.

How can you learn more about your faith beyond Confirmation? Describe specific actions you can take. Then write a brief prayer committing to taking the steps you have identified.

YOUR TURN

A **Complete** the sentences with words from the box. Not all words will be used.

sacramentals	conscience	Incarnation
Divine Revelation	Holy Orders	free will
Matrimony	Virtue	Lord's Prayer
New Law	prayer	Eucharist

1 The _____ is the mystery of Jesus Christ, the divine Son of God, becoming man.

2 The _____ is the law of love taught by Jesus in the Gospels.

3 Our internal sense to judge what is morally right or wrong is called our _____ .

4 The _____ is a summary of the whole Gospel, because it expresses all that the Scriptures reveal about God and about his plan of salvation.

5 Liturgy is the official public worship of the Church, whose center and most intense expression is the _____ .

6 The sacrament by which a baptized man and a baptized woman form a lifelong covenant to love each other and care for their children is the Sacrament of _____ .

7 Like any good conversation, _____ requires talking as well as listening to God.

8 _____ are objects or actions that signify spiritual effects that we obtain through the sacraments.

9 God's gift of gradually making himself known to us is called _____ .

10 _____ is a disposition to do good that directs our actions and guides our conduct.

B **Circle** the letter of the correct answer.

11 The central mystery of our Christian faith is the mystery of _____ , one God in Three Divine Persons.

a the Ascension
b the Blessed Trinity
c the Holy Spirit
d the Incarnation

12 The suffering, death, Resurrection, and Ascension of Jesus Christ are called the _____ .

a the Paschal Mystery
b transubstantiation
c the Assumption
d *Theotokos*

13 The Theological Virtues are _____ .

a Prudence, Justice, Fortitude, and Temperance
b Counsel, Fortitude, and Knowledge
c Charity, Joy, and Peace
d Faith, Hope, and Charity

14 The _____ greatest participation in God's work of salvation can be witnessed in the New Testament, beginning with the Incarnation.

a saints'
b Apostles'
c Holy Spirit's
d Gospel writers'

15 The Marks of the Church are that she is _____ .

a Holy, Catholic, Universal, and Apostolic
b One, Holy, Catholic, and Apostolic
c One, Holy, and Catholic
d Holy and Apostolic

16 Sacred Scripture and _____ , containing all the truths that Christ revealed and entrusted to the Church through his Apostles, form the Deposit of Faith.

a the Epistles
b the Gospels
c Tradition
d Divine Revelation

17 The doctrine of _____ affirms that Mary was free from Original Sin from the moment she was conceived.

a the Immaculate Conception
b the Assumption
c the Blessed Trinity
d *Theotokos*

18 Jesus gave _____ the authority to act as mother and teacher to all the faithful.

a the Vatican
b priests and other religious
c the Communion of Saints
d the Church

19 The Sacraments of Christian Initiation, through which we enter into full membership in the Church, are _____ .

a Confirmation, Eucharist, and Penance
b Baptism, Confirmation, and Eucharist
c Baptism and Penance
d Penance, Eucharist, and Confirmation

20 We are required to participate in the celebration of Mass on Sundays and _____ .

a other Holy Days of Obligation
b Christmas
c the Feasts of Easter and Pentecost
d Ash Wednesday

1973
Roe v. Wade brought before the U.S. Supreme Court; abortion legalized

2008
First African-American elected President of the United States

1978
Election of John Paul II to the Papacy

9
anding

1964
ent Johnson
ivil Rights Act
of 1964

1986
Pope John Paul celebrates first World Youth Day

1991
Collapse of Soviet Union; end of Communist Regime

2005
Pope John Paul II dies/ Benedict XVI elected Pope

62–1965
cond Vatican
Council

1993
European Union Established

2001
Attack on World Trade Center and Pentagon

N T

1955-1968
Civil Rights Movement

1994
Rwandan Holocaust

2000
John Paul II visits the Holy Land

MODERN
AD 1800 – 1945

CONTEMPORARY
AD 1945 – Present

n signs
val Act;
relocate

1929
Lateran Treaty establishes Vatican City as sovereign state

1928
Bacteriologist Alexander Fleming discovers Penicillin

39
Americans'
Southeast
klahoma

1920
Nineteenth Amendment gives women the right to vote

1-1865
Civil War

1914-1919
World War I

1903
Wright brothers' first successful airplane flight at Kitty Hawk, N.C.

1939-1945
World War II

Images: Clockwise from left – The Crosiers, Bridgeman Art Library, The Granger Collection, Bridgeman Art Library, Shutterstock, Bridgeman Art LIbrary, Catholic News Service (3), Shutterstock, Bridgeman Art Library (7), The Crosiers, The Granger Collection, Shutterstock (2)

The Church and Wester

Education and Learning

Historians often describe the sixth through the eleventh centuries as the monastic centuries of education. This is because when the Roman Empire in the West fell in A.D. 476, the social breakdown of society meant that the institutions of learning also dissolved. The monasteries of Western Europe assumed the tasks of learn-ing. In his rule for the Bene-dictines, Benedict of Nursia had prescribed fixed hours of the day for divine reading. This meant that monasteries needed libraries stocked with books—books hand-copied by the monks themselves—and that monks be literate. Since monasteries frequently pro-vided the only schooling in a region, the monks were often also called to educate neighboring children. Through their emphasis

Medieval illuminated manuscript showing a master with a gathering of students

on personal scholarship and their contribution to the education of the laity, monasteries left a lasting imprint on the character of learning throughout the Middle Ages.

The University S

Colleges and universities as them today, with faculties, co study, examinations, and the of degrees, both graduate and graduate, can be traced back Middle Ages, starting with the oping of the universities at Pa Bologna, Oxford and Cambrid the twelfth century. These be cathedral schools, run under pices of a local bishop, or as ir gatherings of masters—often friars or clerics—and students Church fostered the university granting of charters. Because had authority over all of Chris universities typically had to tu them for the right to grant de the early sixteenth century, m eighty universities had been g charters in Western Europe. N these universities still exist to

Charity and Humanitarianism

From the early days of the Church, charity and care for those in need were closely bound up with the Christian life. Early on, the faithful placed offerings for the poor at the altar during Mass. The Church also took up collections from the faithful to provide for the care of the poor. Early Christians would often fast and consecrate the money they would have spent on food as sacrifi-cial offerings. The early Church instituted the care of widows and orphans and provided for the needs of the sick, especially during epidemics. By the fourth century the Church had begun to estab-lish hospitals on a large scale, so that nearly every large city had one. The Church's commitment to the care of those in need has been constant throughout history. Through religious orders, mis-sionaries, and the laity, its work of charity continues to extend to all aspects of society, from healthcare, to education, to humani-tarian aid in countless forms.

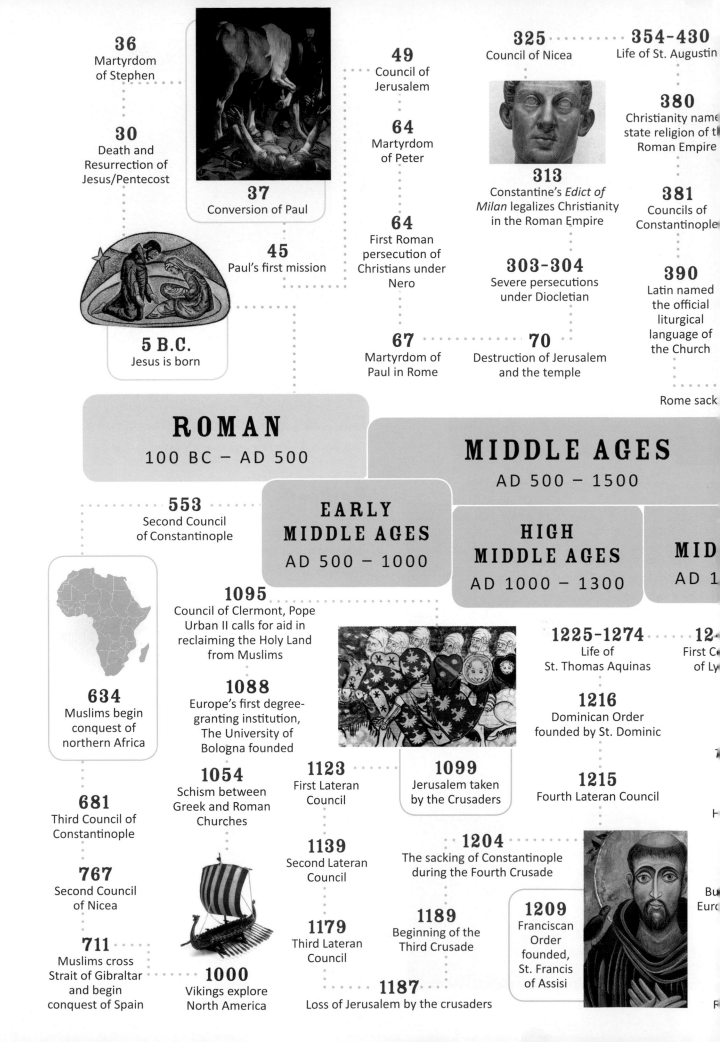

36
Martyrdom of Stephen

30
Death and Resurrection of Jesus/Pentecost

37
Conversion of Paul

45
Paul's first mission

5 B.C.
Jesus is born

49
Council of Jerusalem

64
Martyrdom of Peter

64
First Roman persecution of Christians under Nero

67
Martyrdom of Paul in Rome

70
Destruction of Jerusalem and the temple

325
Council of Nicea

354-430
Life of St. Augustin

313
Constantine's *Edict of Milan* legalizes Christianity in the Roman Empire

303-304
Severe persecutions under Diocletian

380
Christianity name state religion of th Roman Empire

381
Councils of Constantinople

390
Latin named the official liturgical language of the Church

Rome sack

ROMAN
100 BC – AD 500

MIDDLE AGES
AD 500 – 1500

553
Second Council of Constantinople

EARLY MIDDLE AGES
AD 500 – 1000

HIGH MIDDLE AGES
AD 1000 – 1300

MID
AD 1

1095
Council of Clermont, Pope Urban II calls for aid in reclaiming the Holy Land from Muslims

1088
Europe's first degree-granting institution, The University of Bologna founded

634
Muslims begin conquest of northern Africa

1054
Schism between Greek and Roman Churches

1123
First Lateran Council

1099
Jerusalem taken by the Crusaders

1225-1274
Life of St. Thomas Aquinas

12
First C of Ly

1216
Dominican Order founded by St. Dominic

1215
Fourth Lateran Council

681
Third Council of Constantinople

767
Second Council of Nicea

711
Muslims cross Strait of Gibraltar and begin conquest of Spain

1139
Second Lateran Council

1179
Third Lateran Council

1000
Vikings explore North America

1204
The sacking of Constantinople during the Fourth Crusade

1189
Beginning of the Third Crusade

1187
Loss of Jerusalem by the crusaders

1209
Franciscan Order founded, St. Francis of Assisi

Bu Euro

Art

It is hard to imagine art without the great works of the Renaissance masters, such as Michelangelo, Raphael, da Vinci, and Botticelli. Often, the subject of the paintings and sculptures of these great artists were inspired by the Church and the Catholic faith. But it was not just for their subject matter that the artists of the Renaissance are indebted to the Church. During the Renaissance, the Church was the greatest benefactor of the arts in Western Europe. The Popes, especially Julius II (1443–1513) and Leo X (1475–1521), were great patrons of the arts, commissioning artists to create some of the world's most renowned masterpieces.

Leonardo da Vinci, *Virgin of the Rocks,* oil on panel, 1483-1486, Louvre, Paris

roduced under the patronage of the
hitectural treasures are also rooted in
nown as the High Middle Ages, from
h architecture emerged. Known as
minant style for the building of
Key features of Gothic archi-
rior supports that sup-
nted arches, and elabo-
at church built in
f St. Denis, just
churches
ce,

The colonnade at St. Peter's Square in Rome, constructed 1656–1667

Medieval astronomical clock, located in Prague

Science

Did you know that one of the oldest astronomical research institutions in the world is the Vatican Observatory? The Catholic Church has a long history of promoting scientific study and research. In the seventeenth and eighteenth centuries, cathedrals in Bologna, Florence, Paris, and Rome were constructed to function as solar observatories, and possessed the most precise instruments for observing the sun's apparent motion. Individual contributions to the sciences include many by the Jesuits, a religious order founded by Saint Ignatius of Loyola in the sixteenth century. Jesuit priests and scientists can be credited with achievements in diverse scientific fields, including the development of the barometer and the reflecting telescope, early theories about the circulation of the blood, and the creation of star maps of the Southern Hemisphere.

Source: How the Catholic Church Built Western Civilization, Thomas E. Woods, Jr., Ph.D. Used with permission.
Images: Far Left, top left; Bridgeman Art Library, Bottom left; Catholic News Service, Middle, left, above; Shutterstock.

we know
urses of
ranting
under-
o the
devel-
is and
e during
an as
he aus-
formal
earned
The
by the
the Popes
endom,
n to
rees. By
ore than
ranted
any of
ay.

Law

Before the development of canon law, or Church law, in the twelfth and thirteenth centuries, nothing resembling a modern legal system existed anywhere in Western Europe. Since the barbarian invasions into the Western Roman Empire, law was bound up in custom and kinship and was not thought of as a distinct branch of learning. That began to change when, around 1140, the Benedictine monk Gratian published his treatise on canon law, known as Gratian's *Decretum*. In this work, he sought to systematically organize all of the Church's laws, presenting them as a single body of thought and practice. This provided a model and led the way for secular governments to codify their own legal systems, replacing the patchwork of regional, customary laws that governed society.

Architecture

Similar to the painting and sculptures
Church, some of the world's greatest ar
the Catholic Church. During the period k
about 1000 to 1300, a new type of chur
Gothic architecture, this became the do
cathedrals throughout Western Europe.
tecture were the flying buttresses—exte
ported the outside walls—tall spires, po
rate stained glass windows. The first gre
the Gothic style was the Abbey Church
outside of Paris. Other medieval Gothic
include the cathedral at Chartres, in Fra
and England's Salisbury Cathedral. All
of these still stand today.

Church and World History Timeline

476
End of Roman Empire in the West

480-547
Life of Benedict of Nursia, founder of Western Monasticism

451
Council of Chalcedon

431
Council of Ephesus

410
ed by Barbarians

1760-1830
Industrial Revolution; machine-based manufacturing redefines human living

1775-1783
Revolutionary War

1776
U.S. Declaration of Independence signed

1759
Voltaire's *Candide* published

1787
United States Constitution is signed in Philadelphia

196
First moon

Presi signs

19 Se

RENAISSANCE AND REFORMATION
AD 1450 – 1650

ENLIGHTENME
AD 1650 – 1800

LATE DLE AGES
300 – 1500

1453
Constantinople taken by Turks

1454
Gutenberg invents the printing press

1455
Printing of Gutenberg Bible

1478
The Spanish Inquisition begins

1607
Jamestown, first English settlement, is founded in Virginia

1599-1601
William Shakespeare writes *Hamlet*

1534
Henry VIII declares himself head of the Church of England

1545-1563
Council of Trent

1859
Charles Darwin writes *Origin of the Species*

1830
Andrew Jackso the Indian Remo 60,000 forced to

1838-18
Trail of Tears; Nativ forced removal from to what is now C

45
uncil ns

1305-1378
Avignon Papacy

1308-1321
Dante writes *he Divine Comedy*

1337-1453
undred Years' War fought in France

1340-1360
onic Plague strikes pe, killing nearly half the population

1378-1415
Great Schism
Rival papacies in ome and Avignon

1414
Council of Constance

1492
Columbus discovers the New World

1506
The building of St. Peter's Basilica in Rome begins

1517
Fifth Lateran Council ends/Martin Luther's Ninety-five Theses

1521
Martin Luther is excommunicated

1519-1522
Magellan leads expedition to circumnavigate the world

1869-1870
First Vatican Council

186
U.S.

1896
First Moder Olympic gam

21 In the Sermon on the Mount, Jesus taught the _____ , in which he described the qualities those who are part of the Kingdom of God must have.

a Lord's Prayer

b Beatitudes

c Parable of the Persistent Widow

d Works of Mercy

22 The _____ guide our relationship with God.

a First and Third Commandments

b first two Commandments

c first three Commandments

d first five Commandments

23 The spiritual union of all believers, who form one body in Christ, is called _____ .

a saints and holy people

b the Magisterium

c Apostolic Succession

d the Communion of Saints

24 The _____ are loving deeds by which we care for the physical and spiritual needs of other people.

a Works of Mercy

b Catholic Social Teaching

c Beatitudes

d common good

25 The Church's Catholic Social Teaching calls us to work for _____ .

a civil rights

b justice and peace in society

c the environment

d national defense

26 Together, _____ build up the Church and make it holy.

a Jesus and the Virgin Mary

b the Pope and the bishops

c Jesus and the Holy Spirit

d Jesus and all the angels and saints

27 The first three petitions of the _____ are focused on God and give him the glory and honor that he is due.

a Lord's Prayer

b Nicene Creed

c Ten Commandments

d *Magnificat*

28 God created us _____ , which means that unlike the rest of Creation, we are both physical and spiritual beings.

a for material happiness

b on the first day of Creation

c in the Garden of Eden

d in his own image

29 Jesus taught us to call God _____ .

a the First Person of the Blessed Trinity

b our Savior

c the Second Person of the Blessed Trinity

d our Father

30 When God gave the _____ to the Israelites through Moses, he revealed his law for all people of all generations.

a Beatitudes

b Ten Commandments

c natural law

d covenant

C **Match** Column A with Column B by writing the letter of the correct answer in the space provided.

A
a. Original Sin
b. meditation
c. Apostolic Succession
d. soul
e. transubstantiation
f. *Theotokos*
g. Holy Orders
h. Penance and Reconciliation
i. Heaven
j. devotion

B

31. _____ everlasting happiness with God and with all people who love him

32. _____ a title for the Virgin Mary that means "God-bearer"

33. _____ the change of the whole substance of bread and wine into the Body and Blood of Christ

34. _____ the sin of the first man and woman, passed on to all people, through which we are weakened in our ability to resist sin

35. _____ form of silent prayer in which we engage our thoughts, imagination, and emotions to understand a particular truth, Scripture message, or other spiritual matter

36. _____ a form of prayer that, while distinct from Mass and other sacramental rites, is part of the liturgical life of the Church

37. _____ the Sacrament through which baptized men are ordained for permanent ministry in the Church

38. _____ the teaching that the Church is founded on the Apostles and continues to be led through their successors, the Pope and the bishops

39. _____ the invisible or spiritual part of a person that is immortal and will live on after death

40. _____ the Sacrament in which sins committed after Baptism are forgiven

Catholic Prayers and Devotions

The Five Basic Forms of Prayer

The basic forms of Christian prayer include prayers of blessing, petition, intercession, thanksgiving, and praise.

- In a **prayer of blessing**, we acknowledge and respond to God's goodness with joy and gratitude. Because God blesses the human heart, we can in return bless him who is the source of every blessing.

- **Prayers of petition** ask God for something specific, such as help in doing well on a test. For most people, this is the most common form of prayer.

- **Prayers of intercession** are similar; however, the requests made are for someone else. For example, in a prayer of intercession, you might ask God to bring healing to someone you know who is sick.

- In **prayers of thanksgiving**, we acknowledge God as our Creator and thank him for his goodness. We can also offer prayers of thanksgiving for specific gifts God has given us.

- Finally, **prayers of praise** express our love for God.

Sign of the Cross	Signum Crucis
	(SIHG num) (KROO chees)
In the name of the Father,	In nomine Patris,
	(ihn) (NOH mee nay) (PAH trees)
and of the Son,	et Filii,
	(et) (FEE lee ee)
and of the Holy Spirit.	et Spiritus Sancti.
	(et) (SPEE ree toos) (SAHNK tee)
Amen.	Amen.
	(AH men)

Glory Be

Glory be to the Father,

and to the Son,

and to the Holy Spirit.

As it was in the beginning,

is now,

and will be forever.

Amen.

Doxologia Minor
(dahx oh loh GEE ah) *(MEE nor)*

Gloria Patri,
(GLOH ree ah) *(PAH tree)*

et Filio,
(et) *(FEE lee oh)*

et Spiritui Sancto.
(et) *(spee REE too ee)* *(SAHNK toh)*

Sicut erat in principio,
(SEE koot) *(AIR aht)* *(ihn)* *(prihn CHEE pee oh)*

et nunc, et semper,
(et) *(noonk)* *(et)* *(SEM pair)*

et in saecula saeculorum.
(et) *(ihn)* *(SAY koo lah)* *(say koo LOR um)*

Amen.
(AH men)

Hail Mary

Hail Mary, full of grace,

the Lord is with thee.

Blessed art thou among women,

and blessed is the fruit of thy womb,

Jesus.

Holy Mary, Mother of God,

pray for us sinners,

now and at the hour of our death.

Amen.

Ave Maria
(AH vay) *(mah REE ah)*

Ave Maria, gratia plena,
(AH vay) *(mah REE ah)* *(GRAHT see ah)* *(PLAY nah)*

Dominus tecum.
(DOH mee noos) *(TAY kum)*

Benedicta tu in mulieribus,
(bay nay DIHK tah) *(too)* *(ihn)* *(moo lee AIR ee bus)*

et benedictus fructus ventris tui,
(et) *(bay nay DIHK tus)* *(FRUK toos)* *(VEN trihs)* *(TOO ee)*

Iesus.
(YAY zoos)

Sancta Maria, Mater Dei,
(SAHNK tah) *(mah REE ah)* *(MAH tair)* *(DAY ee)*

ora pro nobis peccatoribus,
(OH rah) *(proh)* *(NOH bees)* *(pek a TOR ee bus)*

nunc, et in hora mortis nostrae.
(noonk) *(et)* *(ihn)* *(HOR ah)* *(MOR tees)* *(NOHS tray)*

Amen.
(AH men)

The Lord's Prayer

Our Father, who art in heaven,

hallowed be thy name.

Thy kingdom come.

Thy will be done

on earth, as it is in heaven.

Give us this day our daily bread,

and forgive us our trespasses,

as we forgive those

who trespass against us,

and lead us not into temptation,

but deliver us from evil.

Amen.

Oratio Dominica
(oh RAHT see oh) *(doh MEE nee kah)*

Pater noster, qui es in caelis,
(PAH tair) *(NOHS tair)* *(kwee)* *(es)* *(ihn)* *(CHAY lees)*

sanctificetur nomen tuum.
(sahnk tee fee CHAY tor) *(NOH men)* *(TOO um)*

Adveniat regnum tuum.
(ahd VAY nee aht) *(REG num)* *(TOO um)*

Fiat voluntas tua,
(FEE aht) *(voh LUN tahs)* *(TOO ah)*

sicut in caelo et in terra.
(SEE koot) *(ihn)* *(CHAY loh)* *(et)* *(ihn)* *(TAIR ah)*

Panem nostrum quotidianum
(PAH nem) *(NOH strum)* *(kwoh tee dee AH num)*

da nobis hodie,
(dah) *(NOH bees)* *(HOH dee ay)*

et dimitte nobis debita nostra
(et) *(dih MIHT tay)* *(NOH bees)* *(DAY bee tah)* *(NOH strah)*

sicut et nos dimittimus
(SEE koot) *(et)* *(nohs)* *(dee MEE tee mus)*

debitoribus nostris.
(day bee TOR ee bus) *(NOH strees)*

Et ne nos inducas in tentationem,
(et) *(nay)* *(nohs)* *(ihn DOO kahs)* *(ihn)* *(ten taht see OH nem)*

sed libera nos a malo.
(sed) *(LEE bair ah)* *(nohs)* *(ah)* *(MAH loh)*

Amen.
(AH men)

Prayer to the Holy Spirit

Come, Holy Spirit, fill the hearts of your faithful,
and kindle in them the fire of your love.
Send forth your Spirit and they shall be created,
and you will renew the face of the earth.

Hail Holy Queen

Hail, Holy Queen, Mother of Mercy,
our life, our sweetness, and our hope!
To you do we cry,
poor banished children of Eve;
to you do we send up our sighs,
mourning and weeping in this vale of tears.
Turn, then most gracious advocate,
your eyes of mercy toward us;
and after this our exile,
show to us the blessed fruit of your womb, Jesus.
O clement, O loving, O sweet Virgin Mary!

The Apostles' Creed

I believe in God,
the Father almighty,
Creator of heaven and earth,
and in Jesus Christ, his only Son, our Lord,
who was conceived by the Holy Spirit,
born of the Virgin Mary,
suffered under Pontius Pilate,
was crucified, died and was buried;
he descended into hell;
on the third day he rose again
  from the dead;
he ascended into heaven,
and is seated at the right hand of God the
  Father almighty;
from there he will come to judge the living
  and the dead.
I believe in the Holy Spirit,
the holy catholic Church,
the communion of saints,
the forgiveness of sins,
the resurrection of the body,
and life everlasting.
Amen.

The Nicene Creed

I believe in one God,
the Father almighty,
maker of heaven and earth,
of all things visible and invisible.
I believe in one Lord Jesus Christ,
the Only Begotten Son of God,
born of the Father before all ages.
God from God, Light from Light,
true God from true God,
begotten, not made,
consubstantial with the Father;
through him all things were made.
For us men and for our salvation
he came down from heaven,
and by the Holy Spirit was incarnate
  of the Virgin Mary,
and became man.
For our sake he was crucified
  under Pontius Pilate,
he suffered death and was buried,
and rose again on the third day
in accordance with the Scriptures.
He ascended into heaven
and is seated at the right hand of the Father.
He will come again in glory
to judge the living and the dead
and his kingdom will have no end.
I believe in the Holy Spirit, the Lord,
  the giver of life,
who proceeds from the Father and the Son,
who with the Father and the Son
  is adored and glorified,
who has spoken through the prophets.
I believe in one, holy, catholic
  and apostolic Church.
I confess one baptism for
  the forgiveness of sins
and I look forward to the resurrection of
  the dead
and the life of the world to come.
Amen.

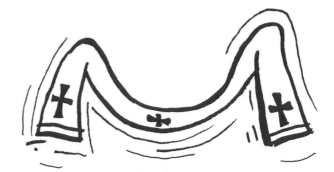

Prayer for Vocations

Lord, show me how to be of service, in your
church and in the world.
Help me to see what you want me to do.
Give me vision, courage, and friends who
encourage me to do your work.
Amen.

Prayer Before the Blessed Sacrament

Lord Jesus, I believe that you are truly
present in the Eucharist.
As I receive you in Holy Communion,
help me to love as you loved,
serve as you served,
so I can be the Body of Christ to others.
Amen.

Grace Before Meals

Bless us, O Lord, and these thy
gifts which we are about to
receive from thy bounty through
Christ our Lord. Amen.

Grace After Meals

Father of mercy,
we praise you and give you glory
for the wonderful gifts you have given us:
for life and health, for faith and love,
and for this meal we have shared together.
Father, we thank you through Christ our Lord.
Amen.

Memorare

Remember, O most gracious Virgin Mary, that
never was it known that anyone who fled to thy
protection, implored thy help, or sought thy
intercession, was left unaided. Inspired by this
confidence I fly unto thee, O Virgin of virgins, my
Mother. To thee do I come, before thee I stand,
sinful and sorrowful. O Mother of the Word
Incarnate, despise not my petitions, but in thy
mercy hear and answer me. Amen.

Act of Faith

O my God, I firmly believe that you
are one God in Three Divine Persons,
Father, Son, and Holy Spirit. I believe
that your divine Son became man
and died for our sins and that he
will come to judge the living and
the dead. I believe these and all
the truths which the Holy Catholic
Church teaches because you have
revealed them who are eternal truth
and wisdom, who can neither deceive
nor be deceived. In this faith I intend
to live and die. Amen.

Act of Hope

O Lord God, I hope by your grace for
the pardon of all my sins and after
life here to gain eternal happiness
because you have promised it who
are infinitely powerful, faithful, kind,
and merciful. In this hope I intend to
live and die. Amen.

Act of Love

O Lord God, I love you above all
things and I love my neighbor for
your sake because you are the highest,
infinite and perfect good, worthy
of all my love. In this love I intend to
live and die. Amen.

Act of Contrition

My God,
I am sorry for my sins with all my heart.
In choosing to do wrong
and failing to do good,
I have sinned against you,
whom I should love above all things.
I firmly intend, with your help,
to do penance,
to sin no more,
and to avoid whatever leads me to sin.
Our Savior Jesus Christ
suffered and died for us.
In his name, my God, have mercy.
Amen.

—*Rite of Penance*

The Angelus

V. The angel of the Lord declared unto Mary.
R. And she conceived of the Holy Spirit.

Hail Mary,...
V. Behold the handmaid of the Lord.
R. Be it done unto me according to thy word.

Hail Mary,...
V. And the Word was made flesh.
R. And dwelt among us.

Hail Mary,...
V. Pray for us, O holy Mother of God
R. That we may be made worthy of the
   promises of Christ.

Let us pray;
Pour forth, we beseech thee, O Lord, thy grace into
our hearts, that we, to whom the Incarnation of
Christ thy Son was made known by the message of an
angel, may by his Passion and Cross be brought to the
glory of His Resurrection. Through the same Christ,
Our Lord.
Amen.

The Rosary

The Rosary is a devotional prayer that honors the Virgin Mary and helps us meditate on the life of Christ. We pray the Rosary using rosary beads, which are divided into five decades. Each decade consists of a single bead followed by a set of ten beads. Before beginning a decade of the Rosary, we reflect on one of twenty mysteries. The twenty mysteries are divided into four groups. Each group is prayed on specific days of the week. See below for the mysteries.

Here are the steps for praying the Rosary.

1. Make the Sign of the Cross.
2. Hold the crucifix. Pray the Apostles' Creed.
3. On the single bead following the crucifix, pray the Lord's Prayer.
4. Follow that with three Hail Marys and the Glory Be to the Father.
5. Announce and reflect on the First Mystery; then, on the single bead, pray the Lord's Prayer.
6. On each of the ten beads that follow, pray the Hail Mary. After each group of Hail Marys is completed, pray the Glory be to the Father.
7. Repeat Steps 5 and 6, continuing with the Second through the Fifth Mysteries.
8. End the Rosary by praying the Hail, Holy Queen.

JOYFUL MYSTERIES
(Monday & Saturday)

1. The Annunciation
2. The Visitation
3. The Nativity
4. The Presentation
5. Finding Jesus in the Temple

GLORIOUS MYSTERIES (Wednesday & Sunday)

1. The Resurrection
2. The Ascension
3. The Coming of the Holy Spirit
4. The Assumption
5. The Coronation of Mary as Queen of Heaven

SORROWFUL MYSTERIES
(Tuesday & Friday)

1. The Agony in the Garden
2. The Scourging
3. Crowing with Thorns
4. Carrying the Cross
5. The Crucifixion

THE LUMINOUS MYSTERIES (Thursday)

1. The Baptism of Jesus
2. The Wedding at Cana
3. The Proclamation of the Kingdom of God
4. The Transfiguration
5. The Institution of the Eucharist

The Stations of the Cross

The Stations of the Cross are a devotion that helps us reflect on the events of Jesus' Passion — his suffering and death on the cross. We can pray the Stations of the Cross at any time, but they are most often prayed in parish communities on the Fridays of Lent.

Jesus is condemned to death.

Jesus accepts the cross.

Jesus falls the first time.

Jesus meets his mother.

Simon helps Jesus carry the cross.

Veronica wipes the face of Jesus

Jesus falls the second time.

Jesus meets the women of Jerusalem.

Jesus falls the third time.

Jesus is stripped of his garments.

Jesus is nailed to the cross.

Jesus dies on the cross.

Jesus is taken down from the cross.

Jesus is buried in the tomb.

How to Make a Holy Hour

There are many ways to celebrate a Holy Hour. All that is required is to make ourselves as present as we can be to God. Here are some ideas.

- ✳ **Focus on the offertory we celebrate at each Mass.** We offer ourselves with the bread and wine that is offered to God.
- ✳ **Simply sit in the presence of Jesus Christ in the Blessed Sacrament.** Allow Christ to enter your heart through the silence.
- ✳ **Meditate on Scripture.** This can be done by simply reading from the Bible or following a more formal method such as *Lectio Divina* (see below).
- ✳ **Eucharistic Adoration:** Through exposition of the Blessed Sacrament, we give ourselves the opportunity to meet Jesus face to face. Many churches offer Eucharistic Adoration at specific times during the week or month.

Lectio Divina

Lectio Divina (lex-ee-oh di-vee-na) is Latin for "sacred reading" or "holy reading." This is one of the oldest forms of Christian prayer, and uses Scripture as a basis for meditation. It consists of four steps:

1 *Lectio* (reading): Select and read a Bible verse. Ask yourself, "What does the text say?"

2 *Meditatio* (meditation): Memorize and repeat the verse over and over again. Ask yourself, "What does the text say to me?"

3 *Oratio* (prayer): After God has spoken to you through the first two steps, ask yourself, "What do I say to God in response to this text?"

4 *Contemplatio* (contemplation): Let the verse rest in your heart. Ask yourself, "What is God saying to me?"

Catholic Beliefs and Practices

The Ten Commandments

1. I am the LORD your God. You shall not have other gods besides me.

2. You shall not take the name of the LORD, your God, in vain.

3. Remember to keep holy the Sabbath day.

4. Honor your father and mother.

5. You shall not kill.

6. You shall not commit adultery.

7. You shall not steal.

8. You shall not bear false witness against your neighbor.

9. You shall not covet your neighbor's wife.

10. You shall not covet anything that belongs to your neighbor.

The Great Commandment

(The Two Commandments of Love)

- You shall love the Lord your God with all your heart, with all your soul, with all your mind, and with all your strength.

- You shall love your neighbor as yourself. (Matthew 22:37, Mark 12:28–31, Luke 10:27)

The New Commandment

Love one another as I love you. (John 15:12)

The Five Precepts of the Church

The Precepts of the Church provide some of the most basic guidelines established for us by the Church. Through the Magisterium, the Church teaches moral truths on many specific aspects of how we are to live, and continues to develop new ways of expressing its teachings to meet the needs of a changing world.

1. You must worship God by participating in the celebration of the Mass on Sundays and on the other Holy Days of Obligation.

2. You must confess your unconfessed grave sins at least once a year.

3. You shall receive Holy Communion at least once a year, during the Easter season.

4. Observe the days of fasting and abstinence established by the Church.

5. You are to help support the material needs of the Church, according to your abilities.

The Three Theological Virtues

- Faith
- Hope
- Charity (Love)

The Four Cardinal Virtues

- Prudence
- Justice
- Fortitude
- Temperance

The Seven Gifts of the Holy Spirit

Wisdom

Understanding

Counsel (Right Judgment)

Fortitude (Courage)

Knowledge

Piety (Reverence)

Fear of the Lord (Wonder and Awe)

The Twelve Fruits of the Holy Spirit

Peace

Kindness

Joy

Charity

Patience

Modesty

Gentleness

Self-control

Goodness

Chastity

Faithfulness

Generosity

The Seven Corporal Works of Mercy

- Feed the hungry.
- Give drink to the thirsty.
- Clothe the naked.
- Shelter the homeless.
- Visit the sick.
- Visit the imprisoned.
- Bury the dead.

The Seven Spiritual Works of Mercy

- Counsel the doubtful.
- Instruct the ignorant.
- Admonish sinners.
- Comfort the afflicted.
- Forgive offenses.
- Bear wrongs patiently.
- Pray for the living and the dead.

The Seven Capital (Deadly) Sins

- Pride
- Covetousness (Avarice)
- Lust
- Anger
- Gluttony
- Envy
- Sloth

The Four Last Things

- Death
- Hell
- Judgment
- Heaven

Four Marks of the Church

- One
- Catholic
- Holy
- Apostolic

The Beatitudes

Jesus taught us the Beatitudes during the Sermon on the Mount. Here is a brief summary of what it means to put them into practice.

Blessed are the poor in spirit, for theirs is the kingdom of Heaven.	Obey God and trust in his goodness.
Blessed are they who mourn, for they will be comforted.	Help those who are in sorrow or are suffering.
Blessed are the meek, for they will inherit the land.	Be gentle and patient with others; try to please God above all else.
Blessed are they who hunger and thirst for righteousness, for they will be satisfied.	Be just with all people; share with those in need.
Blessed are the merciful, for they will be shown mercy.	Forgive those who have offended or hurt you.
Blessed are the clean of heart, for they will see God.	Keep God first in your heart; love God and love others.
Blessed are the peacemakers, for they will be called children of God.	Work to bring God's peace to others, from your own family to those struggling with conflict in faraway places.
Blessed are they who are persecuted for the sake of righteousness, for theirs is the kingdom of Heaven.	Do what is right even when it is unpopular or when it requires sacrifice.

Seven Key Themes of Catholic Social Teaching

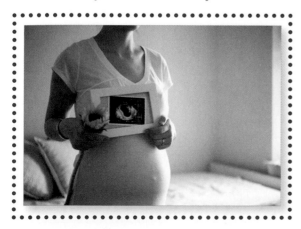

- Life and Dignity of the Human Person
- Call to Family, Community, and Participation
- Rights and Responsibilities
- Option for the Poor and Vulnerable
- The Dignity of Work and the Rights of Workers
- Solidarity
- Care for God's Creation

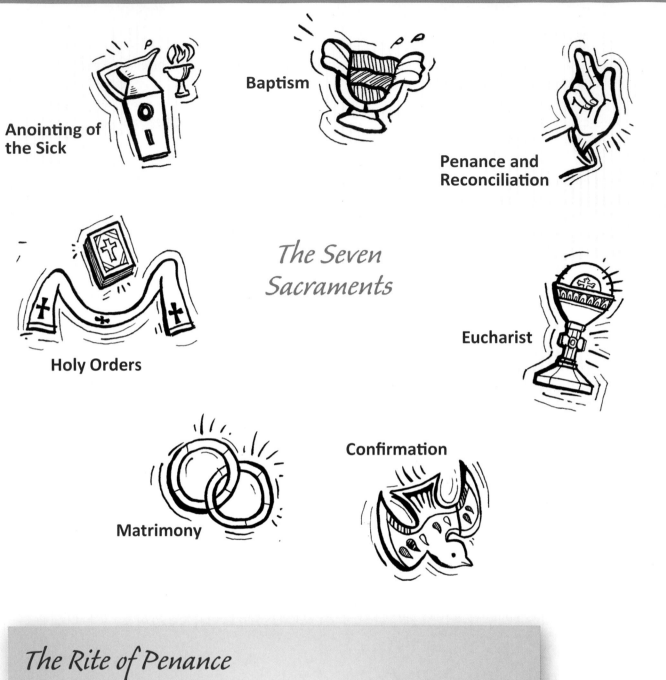

Anointing of
the Sick

Baptism

Penance and
Reconciliation

The Seven Sacraments

Holy Orders

Eucharist

Matrimony

Confirmation

The Rite of Penance

- Preparation of Priest and Penitent
- Examination of Conscience (see page 210)
- Rite of Reconciliation
- Priest's Welcome
- Reading from Scripture
- Confession
- Act of Contrition (Prayer of Sorrow) (see page 201)
- Absolution
- Prayer of Praise and Dismissal

Order of the Mass

Introductory Rites

Entrance Chant

Greeting

Penitential Act

Kyrie (Lord, Have Mercy)

Gloria

Collect (Opening Prayer)

Liturgy of the Word

First Reading

Responsorial Psalm

Second Reading

Gospel Acclamation

Gospel Reading

Homily

Profession of Faith

Prayer of the Faithful

Liturgy of the Eucharist

Presentation and Preparation of the Gifts

Prayer over the Offerings

Eucharistic Prayer

Sanctus (Holy, Holy, Holy)

Communion Rite

The Lord's Prayer

Sign of Peace

Agnus Dei (Lamb of God)

Communion

Communion Song

Period of Silence or Song of Praise

Prayer after Communion

Concluding Rites

Final Blessing

Dismissal

Holy Days of Obligation

- Solemnity of the Blessed Virgin Mary, the Mother of God, January 1
- Ascension of the Lord, forty days after Easter
- Assumption of the Blessed Virgin Mary, August 15
- All Saints' Day, November 1
- Immaculate Conception of the Blessed Virgin Mary, December 8
- Christmas, December 25

An Examination of Conscience for Teens Based on the Ten Commandments

1 **I am the LORD your God. You shall not have other gods besides me.** Do I worry about money, possessions, or being popular more than my faith in God? Do I use tarot cards, ouija boards, or horoscopes? Do I wear a crucifix or other Christian symbols for religious reasons, or simply as jewelry?

2 **You shall not take the name of the LORD, your God, in vain.** Do I curse or swear using the name of God, Jesus, Mary, the saints, or the Bible? Do I speak in a negative way about the Catholic Church?

3 **Remember to keep holy the Sabbath day.** Do I go to Mass faithfully every Sunday and on Holy Days of Obligation? Do I do my best to participate in the Mass by praying the prayers and the responses? Do I avoid unnecessary work or activities on Sundays?

4 **Honor your father and mother.** Do I speak to my parents and other adults in authority in a respectful manner? Do I listen respectfully to them, even when I don't agree with a decision they make?

5 **You shall not kill.** Do I respect human life in all its stages? Do I hurt myself physically or emotionally on purpose? Do I hurt people with the words I say? Do I treat others with violence or hostility in word or in action?

6 **You shall not commit adultery.** Do I look at any form of pornography (online, movies, magazines, etc.)? Do I engage in sexual activity outside of marriage? Do I treat my own body and the bodies of others with respect?

7 **You shall not steal.** Do I download or share music and other media files illegally? When someone asks to copy my homework, do I let them?

8 **You shall not bear false witness against your neighbor.** Have I intentionally damaged another person's reputation? Do I make fun of others, either in person or online? Do I gossip or lie about others, thus hurting their reputation?

9 **You shall not covet your neighbor's wife.** Do I choose clothing that is overly sexualized? Do I wear clothing displaying sexual or offensive messages? Am I modest in my dress, language, and conduct?

10 **You shall not covet anything that belongs to your neighbor.** Do I have an intense desire to have the things my friends have, such as the latest cell phone or video game system? When I see celebrities or others who live extravagantly, do I obsess about wanting the things they have?

Pope John Paul II and the Theology of the Body

The early and middle years of the twentieth century saw a confluence of movements and ideologies that all, to varying degrees, resulted in a skewed understanding of the human person. These include political systems like National Socialism, Fascism, and Communism; the so-called "sexual revolution" and "women's liberation movement"; the rise of moral relativism and the concurrent emergence of "person-centered ethics"; the advent of readily available forms of artificial birth control; and the general skepticism that began to pervade theology and philosophy in the previous two centuries. By the 1960s and 1970s, this had begun to spill over into a debate, both within and outside the Church, about the very validity of the Church's teachings on marriage, sex, and sexuality.

Shortly after his election to the papacy, Pope John Paul II began to address these issues. Beginning in 1979 and concluding five years later, John Paul II devoted 129 of his Wednesday "general audiences" to presenting, the Church's understanding of the human person as an integrated whole—body, soul, and spirit. This extensive series of catechetical talks became known, collectively, as the Theology of the Body. Among the topics he addressed are the question of our ultimate destiny; the creation of persons as male and female; the fall of Adam and Eve, and its consequences for the history of humanity; the complementarity of the sexes; the reality of marriage as a God-given institution, and its role as a reflection of the relationship of the Blessed Trinity; the purpose and meaning of celibate vocations (the priesthood and consecrated religious life) in relation to marriage; and the true meaning of love.

In a sense, the Theology of the Body was the fruit of John Paul's own mature understanding of the human person, formed as much by his own intellect as by the experience of growing up and preparing for the priesthood under an oppressive regime that was hostile to the core tenets of the Faith. It also laid the groundwork for a central theme of his pontificate: the inherent dignity of the human person. The Theology of the Body challenged—and continues to challenge—the world to see the essential beauty of each person, the splendor of the Sacrament of Marriage as a living sign of God's infinite love, and the Church's positive vision for the destiny of all people.

What are the practical implications of the Theology of the Body for teens? Here are some ideas.

❀ The foundation of every relationship in our lives—whether it be with parents, siblings, relatives, friends—is the love that God has for each of us, revealed to us in Christ. This is the focal point of everything that Pope John Paul tried to express in the Theology of the Body. If we keep our eyes focused on Christ, then everything else will fall into place.

❀ If you want others to treat you and your body with respect, you have to set the tone. You know two of the standards: Don't abuse your body with drugs or alcohol. But there are other, equally sinister things to avoid. The practice of self-mutilation has become all too common of a problem—but that doesn't make it okay. Your body is the temple of the Holy Spirit. Other people won't respect it that way if you don't.

❀ You may have heard the saying that "appearance is everything." That's often true, but in more ways than we may think. The way you dress says a lot about who you are, and conveys that to others. Dressing modestly says to others that you respect yourself and them. On the other hand, clothing that leaves little to the imagination can have the opposite effect. If you don't want others to gawk or stare at you, then be sure to give them little to look at in the first place!

❀ The gift of sexuality is one of God's great gifts to us. But it, too, is open to misuse. One of the greatest temptations today is pornography. Twenty years ago, "looking at porn" meant having to go to the corner newsstand and laying out $4 or $5 for a magazine with lots of pictures and little text. Even then, there was the shame of having to carry that magazine in a brown paper bag, so that everyone knew what was inside. Today, pornography is as available as the closest computer. Because it's so readily accessible, it's become more acceptable. But pornography cheapens us and others, and encourages us not to look at others as persons, created in God's image, but as objects for our own pleasure.

❀ Pornography is just one of many sexual temptations that we have to face. Others include sexual relations before marriage (and that doesn't mean just intercourse); use of artificial birth control; masturbation; and any other thing or practice that diminishes the dignity of the sexual relationship between a husband and a wife.

❀ Whether we realize it or not, the mainstream media establishes a certain "image" that everyone thinks they have to live up to. Frequently, that image runs counter to the virtues extolled in the gospel. Remember: The most important image we should be concerned about is God's image. Why? Because that's the image in which each of us was created!

Fasting and Abstinence Regulations

To mark days of special importance during the Liturgical Year, the Church requires us to observe rules of fasting and abstinence. In so doing, we perform penance for our sins and share in Jesus' suffering in his sacrifice on the cross.

Ash Wednesday and Good Friday are days of fast and abstinence. Fridays of Lent are also days of abstinence. In addition, the Church encourages us to practice some form of penance on all Fridays throughout the year. This may include fasting or abstinence, almsgiving or other acts of charity, or other forms of personal sacrifice.

Fasting

Those eighteen years of age and older, and who have not yet celebrated their sixtieth birthday, are required to observe days of fast.

On a fast day, one full meal is allowed. Two other meals, sufficient to maintain strength, may be taken according to each one's needs, but together they should not equal another full meal. Eating between meals is not permitted, but liquids, including milk and juices, are allowed.

Abstinence

Days of abstinence must be observed by those aged fourteen and older.

On days of abstinence, no meat is allowed. Exceptions are made when one's health or ability to work would be seriously affected.

Vatican II

Throughout the history of the Church, popes have called general *councils*—also called ecumenical councils, from the Greek word *oikoumene,* meaning "the whole world"—gatherings of all of the Church's bishops for the purpose of discussing a specific problem or situation and then determining how best to address it.

There have been twenty-one such general councils in the history of the Church, but few have been as far-reaching, and as misunderstood, as the twenty-first and most recent, commonly known as *Vatican Council II*, which was held in several sessions, from 1962 to 1965.

At the council, bishops from all over the world, aided by a wide of variety of experts in various areas of Church life, worked to fulfill the hopes of Pope Blessed John XXIII to bring renewal to the Church and to help Catholics to proclaim the timeless truths of the Gospel in ways that would be most meaningful to the modern world.

The initial fruit of Vatican II was in the sixteen documents approved by the bishops. Of these, the *Constitution on the Sacred Liturgy (Sacrosanctum Concilium),* or *CSL,* has probably had the most far-reaching impact of any of the council's documents. The overriding aim of the *CSL* was to foster the "full and active participation by all the people" in the Church's liturgy. It reaffirmed that while the mysteries of the liturgy remain ageless and unchanging, they must still be offered in ways that are most understood by today's people. For example, the *CSL* paved the way for the Mass to be celebrated in local languages, or the vernacular.

The council used the *Dogmatic Constitution on the Church (Lumen Gentium)* to remind Catholics that the Church is the Mystical Body of Christ and has a hierarchical structure (with the Holy Father as the head). The *Pastoral Constitution on the Church in the Modern World (Gaudium et Spes)* describes how the Church's teachings relate to "the joys and the hopes, the griefs and the anxieties of the men of this age." [*GS*, 1] The "griefs and the anxieties" included the challenges of war and peace in the nuclear era.

Universal religious rights also found expression in the *Declaration on Religious Freedom (Dignitatis Humanae).* Written with the encouragement especially of the American bishops, it affirmed the rights of each person to have freedom to believe in God and to worship according to his or her conscience.

Christ's expressed wish "that all may be one" resulted in the "Decree on Ecumenism" *(Unitatis Redintegratio)* that showed how Catholics can engage in outreach with separated Christian churches and communities, including joint charitable work and common prayer. Similarly, the *Declaration on the Relationship of the Church to Non-Christian Religions (Nostra Aetate)* provided Catholics with principles for prudent dialogue with other religions in the world, such as Judaism, Islam, Hinduism, and Buddhism.

It is fair to say that in the time right after the council, these documents were sometimes misapplied or misunderstood. Pope John Paul II (1978–2005) made implementing the council in continuity with the other twenty general councils one of the greatest priorities of his papacy, and this purpose has been continued by Pope Benedict XVI. Now, nearly fifty years after the council, we are beginning to appreciate fully its monumental impact on the life of the Church.

The Key Documents of Vatican II

The Second Vatican Council issued a total of sixteen documents: four *constitutions*, nine *decrees*, and three *declarations*. These teachings touch upon nearly every area of the Church's life, including the liturgy (the Church's worship); the relationship of the Church to other faith communities and the world at large; the life and ministry of priests, the renewal of the religious communities of men and women, and the role of the laity, to name a few. The following are some of the key documents:

Dogmatic Constitution on the Church (*Lumen Gentium,* Nov. 21, 1964) spoke about the Church as the universal sacrament of salvation and her clear hierarchical structure; it also emphasized the role of Mary in the life of the Church.

Dogmatic Constitution on Divine Revelation (*Dei Verbum,* Nov. 18, 1965) offered the Church's teachings on Sacred Scripture and Sacred Tradition.

Constitution on the Sacred Liturgy (*Sacrosanctum Concilium,* Dec. 4, 1963) hoped to bring an authentic renewal of the Church's worship.

Pastoral Constitution on the Church in the Modern World (*Gaudium et Spes,* Dec. 7, 1965) taught about "the more urgent problems of the day" and the answers that only the Church can provide.

Decree on the Instruments of Social Communication (*Inter Mirifica,* Dec. 4, 1963) endorsed the use of communication (such as radio, video, and, in more recent years, the Internet) ethically and as a means to help spread the Gospel.

Decree on Ecumenism (*Unitatis Redintegratio,* Nov. 21, 1964) addressed the Church's commitment to dialogue with separated Christian churches and communities.

Decree on the Apostolate of the Laity (*Apostolicam Actuositatem,* Nov. 18, 1965) encouraged lay people in the Church to take an even more active part in the Church's mission.

Decree on the Ministry and Life of Priests (*Presbyterorum Ordinis,* Dec. 7, 1965) focused on the role of priests in the Church, reaffirmed priestly celibacy, and stressed the need for all priests to be men of prayer.

Declaration on the Relationship of the Church to Non-Christian Religions (*Nostra Aetate,* Oct. 28, 1965) provided Catholics with guidelines for dialogue with non-Christian religions.

Declaration on Religious Freedom (*Dignitatis Humanae,* Dec. 7, 1965) affirmed the rights of each person to worship according to one's conscience.

How to Read the Bible

The Bible, also called Sacred Scripture, is a collection of seventy-three books. The Holy Spirit guided the writers of the Bible. This is why we say that the Bible is the inspired Word of God. Because the Bible is the Word of God, it must always be treated with respect.

The Roman Catholic Bible contains seventy-three books. These are the books that the Church accepted as inspired by God. The process of determining which books would form the canon, or official list, of books of the Bible was completed in the fourth century, with the help of Saint Jerome. Jerome also translated the Scriptures into Latin, from the Greek and Hebrew in which the Bible was originally written. At this time, the Bible was only divided by the books it contains; it was not until centuries later that each of the books of the Bible was also divided into chapters and verses.

The Bible is divided into two main parts: the Old Testament and the New Testament. The Old Testament contains 46 books, starting with Genesis, and the New Testament contains 27 books, starting with the four Gospels. Not all Christian denominations share the same collection of books.

Here are the books of the Catholic Bible.

The Old Testament

The Pentateuch		**Historical Books**		**Wisdom Books**		**Prophetic Books**	
Gn	Genesis	Jos	Joshua	Jb	Job	Is	Isaiah
Ex	Exodus	Jgs	Judges	Ps	Psalms	Jer	Jeremiah
Lv	Leviticus	Ru	Ruth	Prv	Proverbs	Lam	Lamentations
Nm	Numbers	1 Sm	1 Samuel	Eccl	Ecclesiastes	Bar	Baruch
Dt	Deuteronomy	2 Sm	2 Samuel	Sg	Song of Songs	Ez	Ezekiel
		1 Kgs	1 Kings	Wis	Wisdom	Dn	Daniel
		2 Kgs	2 Kings	Sir	Sirach	Hos	Hosea
		1 Chr	1 Chronicles			Jl	Joel
		2 Chr	2 Chronicles			Am	Amos
		Ezr	Ezra			Ob	Obadiah
		Neh	Nehemiah			Jon	Jonah
		Tb	Tobit			Mi	Micah
		Jdt	Judith			Na	Nahum
		Est	Esther			Hb	Habakkuk
		1 Mc	1 Maccabees			Zep	Zephaniah
		2 Mc	2 Maccabees			Hg	Haggai
						Zec	Zechariah
						Mal	Malachi

The New Testament

The Gospels and Acts

Mt	Matthew
Mk	Mark
Lk	Luke
Jn	John
Acts	Acts of the Apostles

The Pauline Letters (The Epistles)

Rom	Romans
1 Cor	1 Corinthians
2 Cor	2 Corinthians
Gal	Galatians
Eph	Ephesians
Phil	Philippians
Col	Colossians
1 Thes	1 Thessalonians
2 Thes	2 Thessalonians
1 Tm	1 Timothy
2 Tm	2 Timothy
Ti	Titus
Phlm	Philemon
Heb	Hebrews

The Catholic Letters and Revelation

Jas	James
1 Pt	1 Peter
2 Pt	2 Peter
1 Jn	1 John
2 Jn	2 John
3 Jn	3 John
Jude	Jude
Rv	Revelation

HOW TO FIND A SCRIPTURE PASSAGE

The Bible is divided into books, such as the Book of Exodus or the Gospel of Luke. Each book is divided into chapters, and each chapter is divided into verses. Below is a page of the Bible showing these parts.

To find a Scripture passage, follow these four easy steps. Try following these steps to find Luke 11:27–28.

1. Go to the alphabetical index page at the front of your Bible and find the name of the book you need (in this example, Luke) either in the New Testament or the Old Testament listing.

2. Find the page number on which that book begins. Turn to that page within your Bible.

3. Once you get to the page where the book begins, keep turning pages forward until you arrive at the chapter number you need. The image at left presents an example of how chapter numbers are typically displayed in the Bible.

4. Once you find the chapter, find the verse or verses you are looking for, using the small numbers within the text. See the image at left for an example of how verses are numbered.

The Liturgical Year

The Church calendar is called the Liturgical Year. The Liturgical Year allows us to reflect on and celebrate the events and mystery of Christ's life. Throughout the Liturgical Year, the Church leads us through a cycle of prayers and Scripture readings that help us recall and commemorate God's work of salvation as it was accomplished through Jesus Christ.

The Liturgical Year begins in late November on the first Sunday of Advent. It is divided into seasons, such as Lent and Advent, centered around the most important events of Christ's life, such as his birth and his suffering and death. The Church's liturgical calendar allows us to observe and honor these events through the Church's liturgy.

Within the seasons are numerous feast days that mark special events in the life of Jesus, Mary, and the saints and in the history of the Church. A number of these days are Holy Days of Obligation, meaning these days are so important we are required to attend Mass.

Sunday, also called the Lord's Day, is our foremost Holy Day of Obligation, and is at the heart of the liturgical cycle. Every Sunday we celebrate Jesus' Resurrection.

Gathered at Mass with our parish community, we give thanks to God for sending his Son, Jesus, and the salvation he won for us through his suffering, death, and Resurrection.

Seasons of the Liturgical Year

Advent

Advent is the first season of the Liturgical Year. It is a time of waiting and preparation for Christ's coming at his birth as well as his Second Coming at the end of time. Advent begins four Sundays before Christmas and ends at the Christmas Eve Vigil Mass.

Traditional liturgical color: purple, to signify waiting

The Christmas Season

The Christmas season is a celebration of Jesus' birth and the events associated with it. The season begins at the Christmas Eve Vigil Mass and ends on the Feast of the Baptism of the Lord.

Traditional liturgical colors: white and gold, to signify joy

Lent

Lent is a period of preparation for Jesus' Resurrection during which we recollect his Passion—his suffering and death on the Cross. During Lent the Church calls us to share in Jesus' suffering through fasting and abstinence, almsgiving and other acts of charity, and through the liturgy and prayer. Lent begins on Ash Wednesday and ends on Holy Thursday evening.

Traditional liturgical color: purple, symbolizing penance

Easter Triduum

The three days of the Easter Triduum begin with the Holy Thursday liturgy and end on Easter Sunday evening. During these three days we recall the Last Supper, when Jesus instituted the Eucharist (Holy Thursday), Jesus' suffering and death to save us from sin (Good Friday), and Jesus' Resurrection (Easter Sunday).

Traditional liturgical colors: red (on Good Friday), to signify Jesus' Passion; white (the other days of the Triduum), symbolizing joy

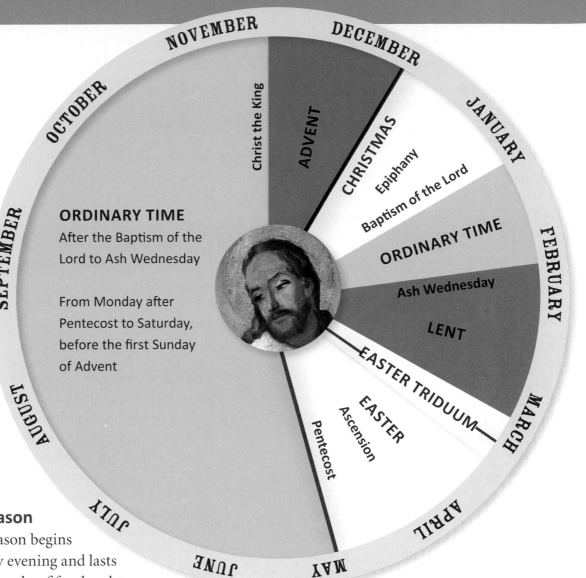

The wheel shows the months of the year around the outside (NOVEMBER, DECEMBER, JANUARY, FEBRUARY, MARCH, APRIL, MAY, JUNE, JULY, AUGUST, SEPTEMBER, OCTOBER) with the liturgical seasons:

Christ the King — ADVENT — CHRISTMAS — Epiphany — Baptism of the Lord — ORDINARY TIME — Ash Wednesday — LENT — EASTER TRIDUUM — EASTER — Ascension — Pentecost

ORDINARY TIME

After the Baptism of the Lord to Ash Wednesday

From Monday after Pentecost to Saturday, before the first Sunday of Advent

The Easter Season

The Easter Season begins on Easter Sunday evening and lasts until Pentecost Sunday, fifty days later. During the Easter season the Church rejoices in the Resurrection of our Savior and in our new life in him. We also celebrate Jesus' Ascension into Heaven during this season.

Traditional liturgical color: white, to signify joy; red at Pentecost to signify the descent of the Holy Spirit

Ordinary Time

Ordinary Time occurs twice in the Liturgical Year: between the Baptism of the Lord and Ash Wednesday (the end of the Christmas season and the start of Lent), and between Pentecost Sunday (the end of the Easter season) and the start of Advent. During Ordinary Time we celebrate and reflect on the events of Jesus' life and his teachings.

Traditional liturgical color: green, symbolizing hope

THE CHURCH'S CYCLE OF SCRIPTURE READINGS

Throughout the Liturgical Year, the Gospel readings for Mass follow a three-year cycle, each cycle drawn from one of the synoptic Gospels, as follows:

- Year A: The Gospel of Matthew
- Year B: The Gospel of Mark
- Year C: The Gospel of Luke

Readings are taken from John's Gospel at various times throughout the year, such as during the Easter season.

The First Reading (usually from the Old Testament) and the Second Reading (usually from one of the Epistles) are also part of the Church's cycle of readings.

Glossary

almsgiving   voluntarily giving money or material goods for the aid of the poor or needy (*page 182*)

Annunciation   the Angel Gabriel's announcement to the Virgin Mary that she was called to be the Mother of God (*page 58*)

Apostolic Succession   the unbroken passing of the mission and authority of the Apostles to their successors, the bishops (*page 52*)

Ascension   Jesus' return in all his glory to his Father in Heaven (*page 36*)

Assumption   the teaching that when the Virgin Mary's earthly life ended she was taken up body and soul into Heaven (*page 60*)

atheism   denial of the existence of God (*page 140*)

Beatitudes   Jesus' teachings about how to live and find real happiness in God's kingdom (*page 156*)

blasphemy   a word, thought, or action that shows scorn for God or the Church or persons dedicated to God (*page 140*)

Blessed Trinity   the Three Divine Persons in one God: God the Father, God the Son, and God the Holy Spirit (*page 28*)

Catholic Social Teaching   the teaching of the Church that calls us to work for justice and peace in society (*page 156*)

chastity   the virtue which regulates our sexual desires, thoughts, and actions (*page 148*)

Chrism   perfumed oil, consecrated by the bishop, used for anointing in sacraments that confer a permanent mark on the soul (*page 88*)

Communion of Saints   the spiritual union of all believers, who form one body in Christ (*page 68*)

conscience   our ability to judge, in accordance with human reason and divine law, what is good and what is evil (*page 96*)

contemplation   a form of silent prayer in which we are deeply focused on the presence of God (*page 168*)

covenant   in Scriptures, a sacred agreement between God and his people (*page 28*)

Deposit of Faith   the unity of Sacred Scripture and Tradition, containing all the truths that Christ revealed and entrusted to his Apostles and, through them, to the entire Church (*page 20*)

devotions   forms of prayer that, while distinct from Mass and other sacramental rites, are part of the liturgical life of the Church (*page 184*)

Divine Revelation   God's gift of making himself known to us and giving himself to us by gradually communicating his own mystery in words and deeds (*page 20*)

Doctor of the Church   a title given by the Church to those whose writings have helped others understand faith or doctrine (*page 22*)

ecumenical council   a gathering of bishops from around the world called together by the Pope or approved by him (*page 134*)

epistle   a letter found in the New Testament, written to the early Christian communities or those who led them (*page 18*)

euthanasia   bringing about the death of a sick, handicapped, or dying person either through a direct action or by taking no action; euthanasia is murder (*page 148*)

evangelization   the proclamation of the good news of Jesus and the love of God through word and witness (*page 44*)

faith   a gift from God that enables us to believe in him and all that he has revealed (*page 20*)

free will   the freedom God gives us to choose between good and evil (*page 122*)

grace   God's loving presence in our lives, given to us freely, to perfect our human freedom (*page 124*)

Heaven   everlasting happiness with God and with the Virgin Mary and all the angels and saints (*page 68*)

Hell   everlasting separation from God, reserved for those who freely and consciously reject him (*page 68*)

Immaculate Conception   the truth that Mary was free from Original Sin and all sin from the moment she was conceived (*page 60*)

Incarnation   the mystery of Jesus Christ, the divine Son of God, becoming man (*page 36*)

Infallibility   the gift given by the Holy Spirit to the Pope and the bishops in union with him to teach on matters of faith and morals without error (*page 52*)

justification   the action of God by which we are forgiven of our sins and brought back into a right relationship with him (*page 124*)

laity   all the members of the Church who are not ordained and who are called to witness to God's love in the world (*page 104*)

Last Judgment   the judgment of all people by Jesus Christ at his Second Coming (*page 36*)

liturgy   the official public worship of the Church, whose center and most intense expression is the Eucharist (*page 80*)

Magisterium   the teaching office of the Church, made up of the Pope and all the bishops (*page 20*)

Marks of the Church   the four characteristics of Christ's Church: One, Holy, Catholic, and Apostolic, as professed in the Nicene Creed (*page 52*)

martyr   a person who accepts suffering or death rather than deny belief in God (*page 142*)

Mass   the Church's prayer of praise and thanksgiving to God the Father and its central liturgy; the celebration of the Eucharist *(page 80)*

meditation   a form of silent prayer in which we engage our thoughts, imagination, and emotions to understand a particular truth, Scripture message, or other spiritual matter *(page 168)*

Messiah   Hebrew word that means "anointed one"; Jesus is the Messiah whom God sent for our salvation *(page 37)*

ministry   based on a word meaning "service," a way of caring for and serving others and helping the Church fulfill its mission *(page 102)*

mortal sin   a conscious and free choice to do something grave against God's law, resulting in complete separation from God and his grace *(page 96)*

natural law   our God-given understanding of the created moral order that forms the basis of personal morality and civil norms *(page 140)*

New Law   the law of love taught by Jesus in the Gospels and fulfilled in his life, death, and Resurrection; the perfection of God's law *(page 132)*

Old Law   the Law of Moses, the Ten Commandments *(page 132)*

Original Sin   the sin of the first man and woman, passed on to all people, through which we are weakened in our ability to resist sin *(page 60)*

parable   a short story that illustrates a moral truth or a religious principle; often used by Jesus to explain his teachings *(page 166)*

Paschal Mystery   the suffering, death, Resurrection, and Ascension of Jesus Christ *(page 36)*

Pentecost   the day on which the Holy Spirit came to Jesus' disciples, with Mary present among them; Pentecost marks the birth of the Church *(page 42)*

Precepts of the Church   obligations established by the Church that all Catholics must observe *(page 132)*

prophet   a person whom God has chosen to speak in his name *(page 34)*

Purgatory   a final purification from sin after death, which one may need before entry into Heaven *(page 68)*

Real Presence   the Body and Blood of Christ truly present in the Eucharist under the appearances of bread and wine *(page 88)*

religious life   a state of life lived by religious sisters, brothers, and priests in community and characterized by the vows of poverty, chastitiy, and obedience *(page 190)*

sacrament   an efficacious sign of grace, instituted by Christ and entrusted to the Church, by which divine life is dispensed to us *(page 88)*

sacramentals   objects or actions that signify spiritual effects that we obtain through the sacraments and that make holy the variety of circumstances of our lives *(page 184)*

Sacrament of Anointing of the Sick   the sacrament administered to the gravely ill, aging, or dying to strengthen them to bear their suffering *(page 96)*

Sacrament of Eucharist   the sacrament in which bread and wine become the Body and Blood of Christ *(page 78)*

Sacrament of Holy Orders   the sacrament by which baptized men are ordained for permanent ministry in the Church as bishops, priests, or deacons *(page 104)*

Sacrament of Matrimony   the sacrament by which a baptized man and a baptized woman form a lifelong covenant to love each other and care for their children *(page 104)*

Sacrament of Penance and Reconciliation   the sacrament in which sins committed after Baptism are forgiven, resulting in reconciliation with God and the Church *(page 96)*

Sacraments at the Service of Communion   the sacraments that are primarily directed toward the salvation of others—namely, Matrimony and Holy Orders *(page 104)*

Sacraments of Christian Initiation   Baptism, Confirmation, and Eucharist, the sacraments through which we enter into full membership in the Church *(page 88)*

Sacraments of Healing   the sacraments in which we receive God's grace for the healing of our mind, body, and spirit *(page 96)*

sanctifying grace   a gift of God infused by the Holy Spirit into the soul, by which we are made holy and restored to friendship with God *(page 124)*

slander   spreading lies or rumors about another person *(page 148)*

soul   the invisible or spiritual part of a person that is immortal and will live on after death in Heaven, Hell, or Purgatory *(page 116)*

stewardship   the responsibility to care for and protect the gifts of creation that God has given us *(page 116)*

Theotokos   Greek for "God-bearer," this is a title given to Mary to affirm that she is the mother of Jesus, who is the Son of God made man, and therefore she is also rightly called the Mother of God *(page 60)*

Tradition   the transmission of the message of the Gospel as lived out by the Church, past and present *(page 20)*

transubstantiation   the change of the whole substance of bread into the Body of Christ and the whole substance of wine into the Blood of Christ *(page 80)*

venial sin   a less serious offense against God's will that weakens our relationship with him *(page 88)*

virtue   a disposition to do good that directs our actions and guides our conduct *(page 124)*

Vulgate   the version of the Bible translated from Hebrew and Greek into Latin by Saint Jerome in the early fifth century *(page 22)*

Works of Mercy   loving deeds by which we care for the physical and spiritual needs of other people *(page 156)*

Index